Interpretive solutions

Harnessing the Power of Interpretation to Help Resolve Critical Resource Issues

Michael E. Whatley, MS

ISBN-13: 978-1-879931-28-2

The National Association for Interpretation is a private nonprofit [501(c)3] organization and professional association. NAI's mission is: "Inspiring leadership and excellence to advance natural and cultural interpretation as a profession." For information, visit www.interpnet.com.

On the cover: Muir Woods National Monument

Dedicated to David Larsen, who supported and encouraged this publication and who has demonstrated that passion, enthusiasm, and commitment can indeed transcend time. David and George Wright both left us all too soon, but they also left a legacy worth nurturing and continuing.

Contents

Acknowledgments

This publication is a joint effort between the National Park Service (NPS), Natural Resource Stewardship and Science Office of Education and Outreach (NRSS OEO), and National Association for Interpretation (NAI). Special acknowledgment goes to Lisa Brochu of NAI who served as the lead editor for this publication. Appreciation also goes to David Larsen of the NPS Mather Training Center, who offered valuable insight, as well as Barbara Little and Teresa Moyer of the NPS Archeology Program, who provided many of the cultural resource examples interspersed throughout this text. Additional thanks go to numerous others who reviewed this document and provided valuable feedback: Professor Susan Jacobson, University of Florida; Angie Richman, communications coordinator for the NPS Climate Change Response Program; Chad Moore, NPS Night Sky Program manager; Theodore Gostomski, science communications specialist at the Great Lakes I&M Network; Dr. Kirsten Leong, human dimensions specialist, NRSS Biological Resource Management Division; Dr. Christopher Mayer, Interpret the World; Dr. Jessica Thompson, Department of Human Dimensions of Natural Resources, Colorado State University; and the many others who helped support, review, and guide this document but are too numerous to list here.

This document is a composite product. The contents are a combination of materials developed by the author and augmented by additional information drawn from public domain materials. Where appropriate, credit is given to outside sources, and gratitude is offered to those behind the scenes who developed supporting materials, as they have added much depth and currency to this publication.

Preface

The Long and Winding Path for Promoting Resource Preservation Through Interpretation

This publication and training manual is about harnessing the power of interpretive communications to improve critical resource protection issues and situations. Matching the right communications approach with the audience most in need of being reached can play a pivotal role in whether a situation stabilizes, improves, or worsens. Appropriate communications can make a positive difference in the role people play in helping to achieve desired resource protection outcomes and results.

The merging of sound interpretive methods with scientifically based resource protection messages is an emerging goal of most, if not all, land protection agencies and organizations. The steady increase of this blended approach is encouraging, and amid climate change, oil spills, unprecedented spread of invasive species, and radical changes to natural fire regimes, it is needed more than ever. The road to get to this point has been long and sometimes arduous, and it is worthwhile for us to reflect on the sequence that took place over time to move this process forward.

Appropriate communications can make a positive difference in the role people play in helping to achieve desired resource protection outcomes and results.

At the onset of establishing national parks, safeguarding resources within them was a paramount consideration. In the 1870s park caretakers focused on protecting wildlife from poaching. Casa Grande became America's first archeological reservation in 1892 following decades of public campaigning for federal protection. Such concerns led to elevated federal legal authority via the Antiquities Act in 1906 to protect archeological sites from looting. In 1916 the National Park Service Organic Act provided additional safeguards, recognizing that both enjoyment and protection were important, but moreover that use had to be subservient to preservation, so that park resources could be left "unimpaired" for the enjoyment "of future generations."[1]

In the early 1920s the first director of the National Park Service, Stephen T. Mather, recognized the need for a professional and academically founded public education program in order to communicate this important mandate. His realization led to the initial stages of a formalized interpretive naturalist service, which in turn led to the development of the organization's first formal wildlife protection programs.

In the late 1920s famed biologist George Melendez Wright,[2] a protégée of the newly emerging naturalist and education initiatives, advanced efforts to more strategically address environmental issues and threats within parks.[3] After completing his degree in forestry at the University of California–Berkeley, Wright started his career with the National Park Service in 1927 as an assistant naturalist at Yosemite. Wright was a promising employee who advanced quickly. In 1929, with the permission of his superiors and use of his own funds, Wright launched a whirlwind national survey of park resources, identifying a plethora of previously unrecognized (or intentionally overlooked) resource threats and needs.[4] In 1932, the Department of the Interior publicized the survey's findings in a landmark report entitled Fauna of the National Parks of the United States, a Preliminary Survey of Faunal Relations in National Parks. With Wright's resource stewardship vision materializing rapidly, in 1934—a mere two years later—he witnessed the designation of a fully funded Wildlife Division within the Branch of Research and Education at NPS headquarters in Washington, D.C. Thus, through his passionate efforts, and with the support of others, the National Park Service began to shift its attention toward protecting natural systems over primarily promoting scenery and, at times, additionally encouraging entertainment (such as developing golf courses, ski areas, skating rinks, bowling alleys, feeding bears, and shooting predators in order to increase elk herds). However, Wright's untimely death in 1936 at the age of 31 due to a tragic automobile accident, and the onset of World War II, stalled many of the fledgling natural resource preservation and protection efforts that had begun to flourish throughout the National Park Service. While cultural resource preservation continued to thrive, in the following four decades only intermittent advances in natural resource management and stewardship would take place. But in the 1980s congressional mandates and other prior encouragements, such as the Leopold report in 1963,[5] spurred the National Park Service to re-commit to advancing its natural resource stewardship efforts—and in doing so, reinvigorated many of Wright's original wishes and desires.

NPS HISTORIC PHOTOGRAPH COLLECTION

Biologist George Melendez Wright in Yosemite National Park, 1929.

During this ensuing interval, natural resource scientists and resource managers increasingly began to recognize, as Mather had before, that more often than not resolution of resource protection and preservation issues requires public understanding, support, and at times positive changes in stewardship behavior. Serving as a pioneer on this front, former NPS Western Region Chief of Interpretation Richard Cunningham addressed this consideration by holding a series of bioregional resource protection communications conferences in the 1980s, linking park areas that shared common environmental themes and issues (e.g., island, seashore, and mountain parks). Resource managers, scientists, and interpreters participated equally in these conferences. In addition, Cunningham, working with other luminaries of the time (such as renowned NPS Marine Ecologist Dr. Gary Davis), initiated a survey of ongoing resource management–related interpretive activities, which provided momentum for further expanding interpretation of natural resource issues throughout the National Park Service.

In the spring of 1987, under the direction of former NPS Associate Director for Natural Resources Dr. F. Eugene Hester, an effort was made to further advance mutual connections between resource management and interpretation. The initiative included the establishment of overlapping Washington, D.C., assignments for two field interpreters, Kim Sikoryak and Mike Whatley. The effort was geared toward investigating ways to merge the powers of interpretation and resource stewardship and resulted in the publication of a series of reports on effective methods for communicating resource issues, the preparation of a variety of resource issue–specific interpretive products, and the first Service-wide workshop on "Communicating Critical Resource Issues Effectively to the Public Through Interpretation," held at Mather Training Center in West Virginia. The team of Whatley and Sikoryak also developed the precursor of the modern-day "interpretive equation," and its sibling natural resource protection "four-step communications formula," which is expanded upon and explained in detail in this publication.

Subsequently in 1988, Congress amended the Archaeological Resources Protection Act of 1979 (ARPA) to focus attention on management actions, including interpretation. Section 10 (c) requires each federal land manager to "establish a program to increase public awareness of the significance of the archaeological resources located on public lands and Indian lands and the need to protect such resources" (16 U.S.C. 470aa-470mm; Public Law 96-95 and amendments to it). Since then National Park Service units and programs have been working to meet that requirement in various ways.

Less than a decade later, in 1994, a report by the Natural Resource Strategic Plan/Natural Resource Interpretation Committee, chaired by Air Resources Management Specialist Darwin (Dee) Morse, offered additional insight into the need for increased support for resource issue interpretation. The report made a number of recommendations, including "encouraging inclusion of funding for an interpretive component for all appropriate natural resource management projects and programs; establishing a Washington Office liaison position between natural resources and interpretation; and developing Service-wide policy support for natural resource issue interpretation."[6]

In 1999, under the direction of then-Associate Director for Natural Resource Stewardship and Science Dr. Michael Soukup, the landmark NPS Natural Resource Challenge came into being. This bipartisan, congressionally supported initiative underscored the importance of science-based decision making, escalated inventory and monitoring programs, and funded an infusion of field specialists and central office experts to provide additional park support. The "Challenge" incorporated all the main recommendations made in the 1994 Natural Resource Interpretation Committee's report and included the establishment of a new Service-wide natural resource Office of Education and Outreach.[7] Currently the Office of Education and Outreach is tasked with coordinating and partnering with a wide spectrum of communications groups and entities. The office, therefore, works closely with the National Park Service's interpretation and education leadership and operates cooperatively with NPS training and development staff and other appropriate governmental and non-governmental organizations.

Today, fully integrating interpretive communications and resource protection is a mainstream practice. This would not have been possible without the efforts of individuals in parks, networks, and central offices; the help of partners such as the National Association for Interpretation, which provided support for this publication and affiliated training materials; and the assistance of indirect supporters, such as the Public Broadcasting Service, which hosted the Ken Burns series on national parks, with specific focus on the accomplishments of George Wright.[8]

Websites Referenced

1. http://www.nps.gov/legacy/organic-act.htm
2. http://www.nature.nps.gov/georgewright/multimedia/podcast/georgewright.cfm
3. http://www.georgewright.org/gmwright
4. http://www.georgewright.org/011thompson.pdf
5. http://www.nps.gov/history/history/online_books/leopold/leopold.htm
6. http://www.nature.nps.gov/educationoutreach/interpretivesolutions
7. http://www.nature.nps.gov/aboutus.cfm
8. http://www.pbs.org/nationalparks
   http://www.pbs.org/nationalparks/people/nps/wright
   http://www.nps.gov/archeology/BestIdea

Introduction

Protected by Artists, Defended by Poets

Dayton Duncan, co-producer of the Ken Burns series The National Parks: America's Best Idea, coined the term "defended by poets." The emergence of the national park idea, its promotion, and perhaps more importantly its protection have been augmented by emotion, passion, and altruism delivered to our society by artists and authors. Henry David Thoreau introduced America (and the world) to the transcendental qualities of nature. Legendary painters George Catlin and Thomas Moran elevated interest in, and love for, the American landscape in ways that had not existed previously. Henry Jackson's photographs of Yellowstone solidified congressional support for creation of the world's first national park. Due to concern over the loss of scientific artifactual data, Mary Hemenway passionately campaigned for the preservation of Casa Grande in the 1880s, while the Colorado Federation of Women's Clubs advocated to protect Mesa Verde—successfully resulting in its designation as a park in 1906. John Muir, "the poet of the mountains," inspired further preservation and protection of many of our most treasured natural landscapes. In the dark years of the Great Depression and throughout the tense years of World War II, American resolve and hope were buoyed by inspirational photographic images by Ansel Adams.[1] Rachel Carson brought new personalized meaning to environmental protection. She once remarked, "If facts were seeds that later produce knowledge and wisdom, then emotions and the impressions of the senses are the fertile soil in which the seeds must grow."[2]

Over the years we have discovered that effective landscape preservation cannot exist without affiliated passion and compassion.

Over the years we have discovered that effective landscape preservation cannot exist without affiliated passion and compassion. The national park concept originated as a uniquely American idea, but it was helped along by social persuasion and public support. Naturalist George Melendez

Wright was as much a philosopher and orator as he was a scientist and resource protection specialist. Hence, over time, when it came to protecting and preserving special portions of the American landscape, the use of both art and science became the winning combination.

As a result of this realization, many of the resource protection issues that our world now faces have led to a renewed emphasis on managing parks and related protected areas through an intentional blending of science, resource management, and interpretation. Today, in many ways, interpreters have become the "poets of our parks" by providing meaningful experiences that touch equally on the hearts and minds of the audience. This role is important and relevant in helping visitors understand what goes into managing resources for the enjoyment of future generations. Interpreters are critical players in this role: they specialize in developing messages that are relevant, meaningful, and memorable.

US FISH AND WILDLIFE SERVICE

Rachel Carson

Many, if not all, park resource protection issues are synonymous with competing human interests. At times the human factor is indirect, such as air- and water-quality concerns generated outside park boundaries that nonetheless affect park resources. At other times adverse human influences are both local and direct, such as inadvertent erosion or trampling of threatened or rare features by trail users, or park visitors inappropriately interacting with or otherwise endangering wildlife. Often, solutions for these problems merely require enhanced public awareness; on occasion, however, individual positive stewardship actions are needed on part of the public.

Resource management specialists, scientists, and interpreters have found they can address critical resource conservation issues more effectively if they work together. Across the country, training courses are focusing on increased networking among professionals to share successful methods and techniques for interpreting significant resource issues.

Between 2001 and 2006 the NPS Natural Resource Office of Education and Outreach hosted a series of resource issue communications workshops focusing on public stewardship and support needs for natural soundscapes, geological resources, ocean stewardship, biological resources, and air-quality considerations. In the late 1990s, an interdisciplinary work group of archeologists and interpreters responded to the NPS Employee Training and Development Strategy to develop a shared course of study so that archeologists and interpreters can be trained together in the skills and abilities needed to carry out effective interpretation of archeological resources. The Effective Interpretation of Archeological Resources: The Archeology-Interpretation Shared Competency Course of Study (Interpretive Development Program Module 440) was finalized in 2000. Four online distance learning courses were developed between 2001 and 2008 and are maintained by the NPS Archeology Program. The NPS Wildland Fire Management program has similarly expanded its interpretive and outreach activities, establishing dedicated interpretive support positions in its Boise headquarters, expanding its internal and public websites and providing wildland fire interpretive training. In 2010 the NPS Learning and Development program undertook the establishment of an interpretive training and development competency related to climate change. The National Association for Interpretation took on support for and distribution of this publication. The NPS Inventory and Monitoring (I&M) program required that networks of parks within the program develop effective public communications plans. In addition, many I&M networks have hired science communications specialists, who have extensive science and interpretation background and skills. In 2010, the National Park Service established a Climate Change Response Program (CCRP) and determined that it was critical to have a dedicated CCRP communications specialist permanently ensconced within that program.

Interpreting resource issues can be more complex than generalized interpretive approaches because of the specific focus on problems and their solutions. This approach includes defining the issue and determining the degree of human involvement in creating (as well as resolving) the issue, crafting effective resource protection messages, determining public support for resource management actions and specific audiences needed to be reached in order to achieve results, and ensuring relevancy of the presentations and techniques used to reach selected audiences (while simultaneously evaluating outcomes throughout the process).

In addition, critical resource issues are most often determined through findings made by scientists and resource specialists. As a result, such issues are generally described initially in a highly technical format. Hence, considerable effort must go into "translating" this technical information into a more understandable context for public consumption. In short, communicators have discovered that regardless of the content, accuracy, or depth of knowledge presented while interpreting critical natural resource issues, the success or failure of the program rests entirely on its understanding and retention by the audience. Growing numbers of field studies and examples demonstrate that through carefully combining scientific knowledge with effective communication techniques, identifying specific audiences, and incorporating other pertinent factors, critical resource protection needs can be met, and successful results can be achieved.

Websites Referenced

1. http://www.anseladams.org

2. http://www.rachelcarson.org

I.

Safeguarding Parks by Weaving Emotional and Intellectual Messages into Effective Stewardship Presentations

Honoring Interpretation as a Longstanding and Essential Management Tool

Interpretation has long been used to promote stewardship of parks and protected areas. It may come as a surprise that this was one of the foremost incentives for the emergence of interpretation during the formative days of American national parks. In the early 1900s Stephen T. Mather, the dynamic (and some would say radical) director of the National Park Service, often ventured out to the parks with the same passion and enthusiasm that we have for these areas today. But during these early days, the primary risks to such treasured resources came in the form of encroachments, inappropriate development, and potential alteration of legislative and regulatory protections. For example, it is not hard to understand John Muir's heartbreak when the Hetch Hetchy dam was congressionally approved in 1914 and eventually built within the pre-existing bounds of Yosemite National Park.

> The challenge today, as it was in the past, is to match the most appropriate method of delivery with the audience most in need of receiving it.

When Mather was visiting Yosemite Valley in the summer of 1919, he was appalled at the competing uses and potential commercial threats emerging in that sacred space. Large numbers of grazing sheep were decimating meadows, unruly commercial tourism facilities were sprouting like weeds, and legislative protection was at risk of being watered down. Mather's distress led him to an idea.

While en route to Washington, D.C., Mather stopped at Lake Tahoe. While there, he attended a lecture by prominent University of California scientist Dr. Loye Miller at the Fallen Leaf Lake Lodge. Dr. Miller was at Lake Tahoe as part of an innovative "nature guide" program developed by Dr. Charles M. Goethe, a prominent West Coast educator, who had seen similar programs in Europe. Mather observed an enthusiastic crowd at the hall where Dr. Miller was captivating his audience with his amazing ability to imitate wild bird calls. The professor's talks on avian "music" were so popular that people often stood by windows outside the overcrowded hall in order to hear him. Mather was inspired by this presentation and soon after collaborated with Dr. Goethe to introduce an experimental federal "nature guide" program at Yosemite National Park in the summer of 1920, using Miller and other University of California scholars as the park's first ranger naturalists.[1] (Development of the naturalist program in the National Park Service: transcript, 1964)

As stated later by Dr. Goethe, Director Mather's strategy was to use the nature guide program to achieve "victory" over the opposition, and "with it he still could translate his national park system dream into actuality." Years later, Dr. Miller confirmed that this was indeed Mather's strategy by remarking, "When folks, after a 1920 field excursion, or at any campfire talk expressed appreciation, the Ranger Naturalist was to explain Washington happenings. Then he was to say: 'if you want a part in this war (on development), send even as little as a postcard . . . .' These poured into Washington, clinching the victory." While this approach would not necessarily be appropriate today, the methods used are noteworthy as they both clearly articulated the issue and motivated people to take action.

It was no accident that scientific scholars were chosen to serve as the first ranger naturalists in Yosemite Valley. However, more than academic knowledge made these individuals successful—they were also extremely effective communicators.

Other pioneers in the field of interpretation, including Enos Mills and Esther Burnell at Rocky Mountain National Park and Milton Skinner at Yellowstone National Park, must be credited with discovering and developing many of the routine interpretive techniques and methods that we take for granted today. From experimental beginnings at parks and protected areas across the continent, early ranger naturalist programs were developed from a blending of academic expertise, field knowledge, and advanced communication skills. The devotion displayed by these initial interpreters led to the celebrated axiom still touted today: Through interpretation, understanding; through understanding, appreciation; through appreciation, protection. According to Dr. Sam Ham, professor of interpretive communications theory and practice, research can now verify that building a stewardship-focused presentation that incorporates these ingredients can be effective.[2] Author Freeman Tilden, who penned the renowned interpreter's guidebook Interpreting our Heritage in the 1950s, made similar observations that are still valid in the current times.

Thus, by skillfully blending appropriate communication approaches with current scientific findings, interpretation can continue to be an effective management option that is used to help fend off significant threats to our parks and protected areas, as well as to the environment at large. Such actions encourage understanding and support for resource management activities and, where appropriate, promote changes in human stewardship behaviors that would otherwise adversely affect critical protected resources. The challenge today, as it was in the past, is to match the most appropriate method of delivery with the audience most in need of receiving it. In parts II and III of this book, we will specifically address four key steps that can assist with successfully communicating current resource protection issues and situations. Indeed, many contemporary examples clearly show how specialized and customized interpretive approaches, if carefully crafted and implemented, can contribute toward achieving positive resource protection solutions.

Identifying the Role of Communications Within the Full Spectrum of Management Alternatives

Interpretive professionals generally find it easy to practice good stewardship activities and actions on a personal basis. However, our goal as professional communicators is to provide motivation for visitors and other stakeholders to find their own interest in and compassion for these same special places and features. More than at any time before, the resources in our parks and protected areas are becoming increasingly stressed or imperiled, making it essential that we foster a sense of understanding, compassion, and appreciation for these resources among visitors and other stakeholders.

The role of park management is to balance competing needs—to honor appropriate public use of parks while simultaneously maintaining protected resources and features unimpaired for future generations. This is a tall order, and it is becoming increasingly important to use the full gamut of tools available to fulfill this mission.

Park management can use many approaches to safeguard parks and protected areas. Some of the more common approaches include setting stricter carrying capacity (i.e., visitor) limits, increasing law enforcement presence and activities, increasing restrictions on (or even closing) public access to sensitive resources, or, when necessary, seeking stronger legislative or regulatory safeguards related to use and impacts on parks and protected areas. However, one of the most economic, effective, and enduring management tools is the use and implementation of effective resource protection interpretive communications (similar to how interpretation assists with educating visitors about safe and appropriate uses of parks and developing their skills to further enjoy parks).

Recognizing the Significance of Persuasive Messaging

Resource stewardship requires that multiple steps be accomplished along with related communications actions. Management issues must be presented appropriately, and solutions must be effectively evoked. If we are successful in using the audience's natural curiosity about resources to create awareness of critical resource issues, we may be able to progressively foster understanding that will lead to taking positive action. A simple analogy can help to further describe this persuasive messaging approach.

Preschool engages natural youthful interests in wanting to learn more. Preschool is also a time to explore and discover. It is a time of curiosity and for awakening our budding awareness of the ways in which people interact and communicate with each other and with society.

Primary school introduces us to basic learning systems such as spelling and grammar, as well as basic math concepts. Progressive advancements in reading and mathematics skills are the goal (e.g., mastering reading and understanding more complex words or advancing from addition to multiplication and division). Education at this point increases our knowledge—from which understanding can grow.

In secondary school and beyond, we focus and refine our mastery of more advanced learning systems. At this point we may go beyond the understanding of our own root language and learn other languages. We may take classes in advanced math. And we often write papers and reports on other societies or governmental systems beyond our own. At this level, we are encouraged to become critical thinkers, to look at matters objectively, and to make balanced and wise decisions that allow us to apply our understanding of what we know.

The persuasive messaging model of interpretation relies on the concept that when we understand something, we are more likely to care about it. Likewise, building effective stewardship requires a similar sequence, based on the belief that if we care about something, we are more likely to care for it. In addition, when the audience is invited to assist in "problem solving" then there is generally elevated buy-in or participation. This model, when applied to resource management situations, has been supported by cognitive and behavioral psychology research.[3]

Interestingly, much social science research suggests that merely learning or having knowledge of a subject alone will not provide the same results. We can teach a student math skills but that does not mean he or she will love the subject or apply it in any way. But the student who understands the relevance of math to everyday life and appreciates it fully can make significant advances in applying it. The same is true in the area of resource stewardship. Individuals who know about a resource may still not care about it, unless they are brought to an understanding of the complexities of the issues surrounding that resource and how it relates to them.[4]

Identifying Common Denominators

Determining a universal understanding of what resource issue communications should be is daunting. Hence reviewing affiliated terms and phrases can provide insight into meanings compatible with, complementary to, and appropriate for incorporation into the resource issue communications process.

In searching for common understanding, the paramount term to review is resource. A park or protected area's resources are the reason for its existence. For the most part, resources refer to physical features such as biological or geological entities, or historical structures or objects. However, resources may also include events, systems, or other more intangible ideas. When a park's resources are threatened, the significance and value of the entire site can also be threatened.

The next key word is issue. In this instance, issue implies risk, threat, or endangerment. Critical resource issues are those at the highest level of risk—if specific action is not taken, the resource's very existence may be at stake. A variety of laws, regulations, and policies safeguard our parks and protected areas. The Redwoods Act of 1978 clearly reminds federal land managers that they have a legal responsibility to respond to resource protection issues in a decisive and proactive manner.[5]

Carefully crafting messages that define the issues and articulate solutions is another important contributing ingredient. Likewise, matching the message with the interests and receptivity of the audience is an equally major consideration. For example, if the selected audience is a group of scientists, then the presenter's vocabulary can (and should) be filled with facts, data, scientific terminology, graphs, charts, calculations, and other forms of academic shorthand. But if the audience is third-graders, the approach should be based on what we know about childhood development and include discovery, surprise, reward, simplicity, reinforcement, and other sensory-based forms of observation and comprehension (while avoiding jargon and overly complex terminology). Likewise, it would be appropriate to interpret differently to an audience of adults who might have minimal background in scientific terminologies or concepts, but who have a significant degree of practical experience and ability to understand complex situations or conditions. Such an audience might require that we avoid scientific jargon, but it may be perfectly acceptable to provide relatively complex definitions and analogies to this group. Additionally, if the audience comprises special interest groups such as hikers, boaters, or hunters, it is important we convey resource protection messages to them in ways that touch upon their own interests and levels of understanding, in both familiar and comfortable ways.[6]

Ultimately, the term problem-solving communications, like other forms of interpretation, implies the need for reaching audiences in ways that are relevant to them while also focusing on improving or resolving resource issues and situations.

Furthermore, problem-solving implies that communication efforts are in sync with and supportive of the agency or organization's mission. This approach is consistent with the National Association for Interpretation's definition of interpretation as a mission-based communication process that forges emotional and intellectual connections between the interests of the audience and the meanings inherent in the resource.

Thus, problem-solving resource issue interpretation specifically addresses resource management issues—and, when necessary and appropriate, engenders positive behavioral actions that help resolve or improve a protected area's resource stewardship or preservation needs.

Addressing Accuracy and Volatility

It may seem odd to mention accuracy and volatility within the same context, but both are of equal importance. One of an interpreter's biggest discomforts comes from working with stale or dated information, especially when he or she hasn't been informed about the availability of more current information from technical subject specialists. In these circumstances, interpreters can unintentionally promote information that is outdated, inaccurate, or flawed, which in turn can present significant problems for subject specialists or, even worse, difficulties for management.

Such concerns can make even the best interpreter reluctant to take on complex or sticky critical resource topics and subjects. But there are ways around these concerns, and the need for providing accurate and compelling resource protection messages far outweighs the temptation to simply shy away from difficult or controversial topics or situations. Interpreters must be adaptable in light of resource issue volatility. In the world of science, hypotheses are constantly being challenged and refined. Likewise, applications of science-based management solutions may vary over time, sometimes gradually, sometimes rapidly.

An example of this sort of volatility can be found within wildland fire management activities. Using sound science to make their decisions, managers in certain areas have determined that it may be appropriate to take actions to restore natural fire regimes and related conditions. These actions might include using prescribed burning under appropriate, well-controlled, and well-monitored conditions. However, depending on a variety of factors (such as potential risk to neighboring communities, air quality considerations, or other unexpected outside issues), prescribed burning may not be selected as the preferred restoration alternative. In such situations, the managers may select another valid approach, which could include manual or mechanical clearing of flammable vegetation materials as opposed to prescribed burning.

An interpreter could be put in an awkward position if he or she were to develop an interpretive product or activity that focused solely on the advantages of and reasons for using prescribed burning to help restore natural regimes when a localized decision has been made to not undertake this alternative. A more secure approach is to focus on the anchor message or concept that underlies the situation or topic. In this case, the anchor message is restoration of natural fire regimes and management's science-based determination that it is appropriate to take action (from among a variety of appropriate alternatives) to help restore or rebalance such situations.

Practicing Concentration Versus Dilution

On the back of one brand of maple syrup from New Hampshire, the label notes, "It takes 40 gallons of sap to produce one gallon of pure maple syrup." Sometimes subject specialists complain that the information provided by interpreters is a watered down version of what they feel, as technical experts, needs to be presented. Perhaps, on occasion, this is true. But when it comes to presenting scientific concepts or technical information, distillation is what we should be striving for, as opposed to dilution or, even worse, saturation.

Once again, the key factor for determining the amount and type of information provided is the audience. Audiences are most receptive to information that is relevant to them. Complexity is not necessarily irrelevant to most audiences; however, overwhelming or inappropriate detail is.

Science-based decision making is dependent upon gathering sufficient data to develop valid conclusions. However, the summary of these conclusions is what managers generally use to make their decisions or to justify them to others. Resource issue interpretation is in a similar situation. The presenter is required to understand and comprehend the details behind a particular resource issue, situation, or story, but he or she is equally accountable for distilling and transferring this information into concepts, terms, and relationships that the audience can understand.

Using Time-Honored and Current Guidelines for Promoting Effective Communications

Interpretation helps park visitors gain inspiration and meaning from their surroundings. Numerous guidelines have been established to help interpreters accomplish this purpose. In many cases the past can be prologue to the future. Therefore, it is occasionally worthwhile to reflect on some of the more prominent time-honored guidelines for promoting efficient interpretive communications. In his renowned handbook, Interpreting for Park Visitors, Dr. William J. Lewis noted the foresight that was evident in developing interpretive guidelines in the early days.[7] Lewis uncovered a series of goals prepared in 1932 by Dr. Harold C. Bryant and Dr. Wallace W. Atwood Jr. of the NPS Education Division. (Bryant was also a University of California–Berkeley fellow and contemporary of the aforementioned Loye Miller and George Wright.[8]) In those days, NPS naturalists and resource managers were one and the same. Their goals were to establish effective resource understanding through the following benchmarks:

1. Simple, understandable interpretation of the major features of each park to the public by means of field trips, lectures, exhibits, and literature.

2. Emphasis upon leading the visitor to study the real thing rather than to use secondhand information. Typical academic methods are avoided.
3. Utilization of highly trained personnel with field experience, ability to interpret to the public the laws of the universe as exemplified in the parks, and ability to develop concepts of laws of life useful to all.
4. A research program that furnished a continuous supply of dependable facts suitable for use in connecting with the educational program.

In the 1950s Freeman Tilden, noted author of Interpreting Our Heritage,[9] developed six benchmark "principles of interpretation" that are still relevant today:

1. Any interpretation that does not somehow relate what is being displayed or described to something within the personality or experience of the visitor will be sterile.
2. Information, as such, is not interpretation. Interpretation is revelation based upon information.
3. Interpretation is an art which combines many arts.
4. The chief aim of interpretation is not instruction, but provocation.
5. Interpretation should aim to present a whole rather than a part.
6. Interpretation addressed to children requires a separate program.

Interpreting for Park Visitors

Interestingly, in the first edition of Tilden's provocative and timeless book, he astutely refers to an even earlier source of guidance. He noted that in 1928, NPS Chief Naturalist Ansel P. Hall (another member of the University of California–Berkeley group) made the following observations about how "neither the function nor the aim of interpretation should be purely to promote instruction. Remember always that the visitor comes to see the Park itself and its superb natural phenomena, and that the museums, lectures, and guided trips afield are but a means of helping the visitor to understand and enjoy these phenomena more thoroughly…" Hall went on to state, "The visitor must be stimulated to first want to discover things for himself, and second, to see and understand the things at which he looks…."

Most, if not all, of these concepts and guidelines are appropriate today for interpreting significant natural resource issues. However, several additional factors must be taken into consideration. Specifically, resource issue communications today must also deal with articulating resource problems and evoking solutions.

Indeed, there are a number of scholars and professionals in current times addressing these considerations. Among these is Dr. Susan K. Jacobson, professor in the Department of Wildlife Ecology and Conservation at the University of Florida. In 2009, Jacobson reissued her laudable and comprehensive text Communications Skills for Conservation Professionals.[10] Her book provides in-depth guidance for achieving conservation goals though better communications. It introduces communications approaches and offers real-world examples to help conservation professionals develop the skills they need to communicate effectively. Specifically, in her publication, she

- describes research techniques for gathering background information and targeting audiences,
- outlines steps involved in developing a communications campaign,
- explains how to use mass media and work with partners,
- provides examples for developing effective interpretive media,
- explores long-term conservation education strategies, and
- presents program evaluation techniques.

NATIONAL PARK SERVICE

Freeman Tilden

Other publications that provide pertinent guidance have similarly emerged in recent times. Among these are Personal Interpretation: Connecting Your Audience to Heritage Resources by Lisa Brochu and Tim Merriman,[11] Communicating Nature: How We Create and Understand Environmental Messages by Julia B. Corbett,[12] Environmental Communication and the Public Sphere by Robert Cox,[13] and Meaningful Interpretation by David L. Larsen.[14] Targeting specific audiences and maintaining relevancy are consistent themes throughout these contemporary publications. In total, these publications have helped take the profession of interpretation to a more sophisticated level. They recognize the value of integrating social science and market research into audience understanding and working toward presenting messages that are measurably relevant to the recipient.

Specifically Defining Resource Issue Interpretation

The art and science of interpretation and its engaging methods and techniques offer a powerful and compelling means for fostering critically needed stewardship of increasingly rare, fragile, threatened, and at times endangered park and protected resources. As human influences and impacts on our protected natural and cultural resources grow, so too does the need to involve citizens in appropriate resource stewardship solutions.

As noted earlier, defining resource issue communications can be daunting. The following definitions provide additional clarification.

The interpretive Definitions Project,[15] which was cosponsored by the National Association for Interpretation and the Environmental Protection Agency (and conducted in cooperation with 24 additional agencies and professional organizations, including the National Park Service), assembled in 2007 to clarify a host of definitions for interpretive terms, activities, and concepts. The definition selected by the project for Resource Issue Interpretation was: "A mission-based interpretive communications process that uses science-based resource condition assessments and findings to deliver specific stewardship messages to target and general audiences with the desired outcome of bringing specific resource issues to resolution." (Definitions Project: 1/23/2007)

The project endorsed an equally important collateral definition (in the form of a formula), which outlines the steps and actions necessary to carry out effective resource issue interpretation. This formula is synonymous with the steps used throughout this publication. The project recognized that the essential ingredients of this formula consist of "identifying an issue, determining an appropriate message, identifying target audience(s), and selecting appropriate interpretive techniques to accomplish resource protection." Definitions Project: 1/23/2007

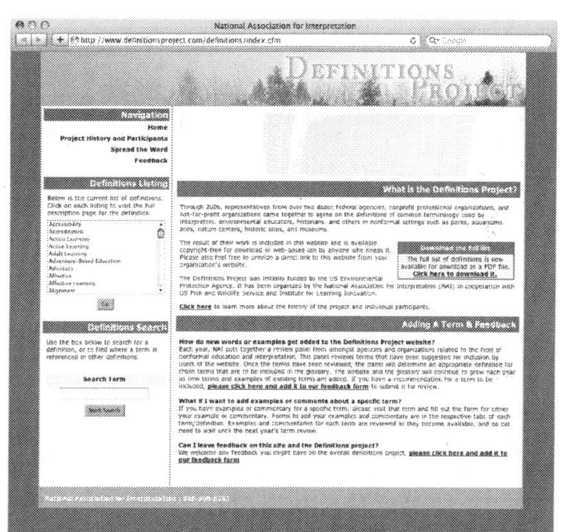

Definitions Project website

A complementary statement validating the importance of resource issue interpretation and education can be found in the 2006 National Park Service Management Policies, which note that "parks should, in balanced and appropriate ways, thoroughly integrate resource issues and initiatives of local and Service-wide importance into their interpretive and educational programs." 2006 NPS Management Policies 1.4.2

In regard to natural resource management, Management Policies further states that the National Park Service "will strive to understand, maintain, restore, and protect the inherent integrity of the natural resources, processes, systems, and values of the parks while providing meaningful and appropriate opportunities to enjoy them."[16] (2006 NPS Management Policies 4.0)

The Definitions Project describes the role of cultural resource management as "the process by which the impacts to cultural resources are considered and the effects of potential impacts are mitigated as required under historic preservation laws and statutes. Management includes protection, stabilization, and interpretation." Definitions Project: 1/23/2007

There is sufficient convergence among these various definitions to assure that current trends and best practices for interpreting resource issues are appropriately being carried out. The common ingredients are (1) assuring that interpretive presentations are relevant and (2) that key audiences are being reached.

Websites Referenced

1. http://www.archive.org/details/developmentnat00bryarich
2. http://www.uidaho.edu/cnr/css/samham
3. http://college.cengage.com/education/pbl/tc/motivate.html
   http://cnx.org/content/m14650/latest/
4. http://www.cnr.uidaho.edu/css487/Philosophy_presentation.ppt
   http://www.cnr.uidaho.edu/css487/Philosophy_presentation.ppt
5. http://www.nps.gov/history/history/online_books/anps/anps_7e.htm
6. http://honolulu.hawaii.edu/intranet/committees/FacDevCom/guidebk/teachtip/piaget.htm
   http://www.learningandteaching.info/learning/piaget.htm
7. http://corpslakes.usace.army.mil/employees/interpretive/refs.html
8. http://www.nps.gov/history/history/resedu/education.htm
9. http://www.nps.gov/history/history/online_books/.../tilden.htm
10. http://www.wec.ufl.edu/faculty/jacobsons
11. http://www.interpnet.com/publications/interppress.shtml
12. http://faculty.utah.edu/u0030575/bibliography/index.hml
13. http://www.esf.edu/ecn/whatisec.htm
14. http://www.nps.gov/history/history/online_books/eastern/meaningful_interpretation/
15. http://www.definitionsproject.com/definitions/def_history.cfm
16. http://www.nps.gov/policy/mp2006.pdf

Developing a Customized Approach to Communicating Resource Issues and Achieving Positive Outcomes

Our parks and protected places face innumerable challenges, and with them come unprecedented opportunities to protect these special places for future generations. A central ingredient of that protection involves the direct efforts of interpreters through their work in educating the public about threatened and endangered resources and related issues in the parks. While some threats to parks (such as climate change and atmospheric nitrogen deposition) may be beyond local capacities to resolve, local efforts can and do make positive cumulative impacts. Other threats can be addressed and improved through local stewardship activities and positive changes in actions, attitudes, and support. Increasingly, natural and cultural resource managers work together with interpreters to address threats facing resources in parks and protected areas, with crucial implications for resource preservation.

> It routinely falls on interpreters' shoulders to explain to the public why problems exist and how the problems might best be addressed.

Time-Tested Examples

The following examples illustrate real resource situations that benefitted from appropriately developed communications solutions. The first came about in an era when developing a standardized process for establishing effective resource issue communications was just emerging. The other examples are more current and demonstrate the benefits of taking steps to engage the public in active stewardship solutions related to critical resource issues.

Example 1: Loggerhead Turtles at Cape Hatteras National Seashore

When natural resource management was reemerging in the 1980s from its unanticipated four-decade hiatus and early efforts were being taken to define effective approaches for using communications to resolve resource protection issues, Cape Hatteras National Seashore was experiencing a problem with people interfering with nesting female loggerhead turtles on the beach. When disturbed, the turtles would go out to sea without laying their eggs, thus interrupting the reproductive cycle. National Park Service staff knew that human activities caused the problem, but it took a few attempts to hone in on a successful interpretive approach. Initial attempts at educating park visitors about the threat failed to produce satisfactory results. After determining that local citizens—not destination visitors—were the primary group disturbing the turtles, the interpretive staff sent postcards, with basic information about the importance of leaving nesting turtles alone, to residents surrounding the park. Reaching local residents proved to be the most effective approach for resolving the issue; turtle reproductive levels rebounded. This situation became a classic example of the importance of evaluating the interpretive approach and readjusting when necessary and of matching the appropriate audience with the most effective communication solution.

Example 2: Snowy Plovers at Point Reyes National Seashore

In more recent times, observations at Point Reyes National Seashore found that park visitors were unintentionally affecting nesting western snowy plovers and their fledglings. The newly hatched birds needed to follow their parents down to the beach to forage for food, but visitors using the beach interfered with the birds' nesting and foraging patterns. National Park Service resource managers and interpreters responded by developing a multi-pronged communications approach, creating displays, public contact programs, and additional innovative strategies to educate surfers, beach users, and anglers (such as providing free dog leashes with stewardship messages on them). The intent was to develop a series of customized communications techniques that were appropriate for (and appreciated by) each of these individual groups. These targeted and innovative interpretive programs contributed significantly to maintaining critical plover population levels.[1]

Example 3: Tree Cutting at Battlefields to Restore Cultural Landscapes

Civil War battlefield and military parks occasionally encounter public resistance for clearing trees to restore the mid-19th century appearance of the landscapes. At Gettysburg National Military Park, brush and trees had taken over historical topographic features related to the July 1863 battle. The lack of an accurate understanding of the features as a result of overgrowth had in many cases led to the loss of important topographical resources. Fields in 1863 were forests in 2001 when the park initiated brush and tree removal. "Witness trees"—trees present at the time of battle—were left in place. The public, however, was overwhelmingly opposed to any tree cutting. To ease the conflict, the park held public meetings, distributed informational materials, and posted a page on its website to educate the public about the issues at stake.[2]

Tree cutting continues to be controversial at Gettysburg and other national battlefield parks, but communications efforts are having a positive effect. In 2008 the National Park Service was similarly criticized for cutting a grove of oak trees at Manassas National Battlefield Park to restore partial sight lines. Tree cutting as a resource preservation tool may seem counterintuitive to some members of the public, which makes the collaborative response by natural and cultural resources managers and interpreters all the more important. Parks need to clearly communicate how and why controversial decisions and actions evolve for the organization to retain credibility and support.

Gettysburg National Military Park

Example 4: Changing Visitor Behavior and Attitudes at Kings Mountain National Military Park and Chickamauga and Chattanooga National Military Park

One problem facing many cultural parks is the impact of metal detecting on archeological sites. Amateur archeologists occasionally disturb the ground searching for bullets, hardware, belt buckles, or other items as a hobby, for personal collections, or for sale. Some of these individuals may not realize their actions are inappropriate and generally illegal or that their digging disturbs the context of the artifacts in sites and damages their potential research value. Since 1992 archeologists from the NPS Southeast Archeological Center have worked with metal detector hobbyists to conduct battlefield surveys at Kings Mountain National Military Park and Chickamauga and Chattanooga National Military Park, as well as other parks in the Southeast. Drawing upon hobbyists' expertise in metal detecting technology and techniques, the program also aims to affect attitudes toward sites and foster behaviors that help to preserve them. As a result of the program, dozens of metal detector hobbyists have contributed to the goal of identifying sites for their protection rather than their destruction thus also helping to reduce erosion, and giving metal detector enthusiasts a legitimate activity that contributes to research.

These examples provide solid evidence that communication and interpretation can improve the public's understanding of the choices made by park managers. It routinely falls on interpreters' shoulders to explain to the public why problems exist and how the problems might best be addressed. Because of its value in helping the public understand and support management actions and potentially change individual stewardship activities to protect park resources, interpretation is a necessity at Cape Hatteras, Point Reyes, Gettysburg, and every park site whether the issues are small or large, imminent or distant. Threats to resources range from spread of invasive species, erosion, and water/sound/air/light pollution to wildlife disturbance, disruptions to natural fire regimes, wildlife population imbalances, and other inadvertent resource disruptions by humans. Such threats affect virtually every park and the natural and cultural resources within them. Larger threats, such as climate change, require even greater interpretive efforts to advance public understanding. It is important for managers of natural and cultural resources to apply interdisciplinary thinking toward interpreting threats to resources. Educating the public is unquestionably one of the most important roles of all land preservation organizations.

The Role of Interpretation in Organizational Stewardship Goals

National Park Service Management Policies recommends that "interpretive programs are the methods the Service uses to connect people to their parks, with opportunities for all visitors to form their own intellectual, emotional, and physical connections to the meanings and values found in the parks' stories. Facilitating those opportunities through effective interpretive and educational programs will encourage the development of a personal stewardship ethic and broaden public support for preserving and protecting park resources so that they may be enjoyed by present and future generations."[3] (2006 NPS Management Policies 7.0)

A key purpose of all park and protected area interpretive and educational programs is to advance the organizational mission by providing memorable educational and recreational experiences that will help the public understand the meaning and relevance of park resources and foster the development of a sense of stewardship. Interpretive programs help to forge connections between resources, visitors, the community, and the park or protected area. Those connections link a park's tangible resources to the intangible values found within the resource so that visitors more readily retain information, grasp meanings, and adopt new positive stewardship behaviors and values because they are directly involved with cultural and natural heritage resources and sites.

Enjoyment of parks is a fundamental part of the visitor experience. That experience can be heightened when it progresses from enjoyment to an understanding of the reasons for a park's existence and the significance of its resources. Virtually every public land management organization is committed to extending its leadership in education, building on what is in place, and pursuing new relationships and opportunities to make parks and protected landscapes even more meaningful in the life of the user.

The art and science of interpretation and its engaging methods, approaches, and techniques offer powerful and compelling means for fostering critically needed stewardship of increasingly rare, fragile, threatened, and endangered park resources. As human influences and impacts on our protected resources grow, so too does the need to involve citizens in appropriate resource stewardship solutions. Gone is the day when we assumed it was enough to simply establish a legislative boundary around a tract of land containing significant features to ensure protection in perpetuity. Today, and evermore into the future, a constant infusion of citizen-based understanding, support, and participation is essential to ensure the long-term survival of these heritage treasures.

In the past, the mission of the interpreter was primarily to foster an appreciation and understanding of basic park values, which, in turn, would lead to public protection of them. Today, to safeguard park resources, the interpreter must also address a multitude of growing environmental threats and other problems, both inside and outside park boundaries.

Some resource subjects or topics can be interpreted primarily from a promotional or inspirational perspective, as they do not have significant issues or problems associated with them. For example, when a park undertakes an extensive All Taxa Biodiversity Inventory (ATBI) or a briefer BioBlitz "snapshot" of park resources, the primary goal is to identify, more fully understand, and document the vast array of living organisms within that particular location. In a similar way, archeological surveys at parks may investigate part or all of a park to identify and document archeological resources. An archeological survey gives resource managers a better idea of the location and array of sites within the park, their condition, and their potential for research. Problems or issues are often not the initial focus of such activities, and an appropriate interpretive follow-up would be to design interpretive presentations and outreach activities that highlight and promote any resulting discoveries and understanding using traditional interpretive approaches and methods.[4]

Advancing Problem-Solving Interpretive Techniques that Foster Positive Stewardship Actions

An alarming and growing number of resource topics and subjects have serious issues and problems associated with them. In these situations there is usually a clearly definable human factor affiliated with the problem, often affecting the health, well-being, or survivability of the resource at risk. Similarly, there are often identifiable citizen-based steps and measures that can be taken to help resolve or improve these problems (and also provide meaningful civic engagement opportunities).[5] Therefore, the human dimension factors related to both the creation of associated problems and the development of appropriate solutions are important to keep in mind. In such situations, additional measures beyond promotional or other traditional interpretive approaches are often necessary. This type of interpretive effort can be referred to as fitting within the realm of problem-solving communications.

In order to effectively interpret—and protect—resources that have significant human-dimension-related problems or issues, four key determinations need to be made at the onset:

- What is the issue (based on pertinent scientific information) and the degree of human involvement associated with creating the problem and developing a solution? (For example, declining plover populations at Point Reyes became a definable critical resource "issue" that had a high level of identifiable human interactive factors that related to both the problem as well as the solution.)

- What are the appropriate audiences that need to be reached (i.e., which has the most influence or effect) in relation to resolving or improving the critical resource issue or situation? (For example, key audiences in the Point Reyes plover example included anglers, surfers, and beach walkers.)

- What is the message that needs to be conveyed in order to communicate beneficial changes in understanding, attitude, or behavior necessary for resolving or improving the particular critical resource issue or problem? (For example, in the Point Reyes plover situation, effective messages that articulate why "plovers need their space" were developed.)
- What is the most appropriate communications approach for delivering the message to the preferred audience(s)? This approach should be in forms that those particular audiences will understand, appreciate, or be familiar with. (For example, specific approaches at Point Reyes were developed to independently reach beach walkers, surfers, and fishermen, while at the Kings Mountain the park creatively reached out to metal detector hobbyists for support and cooperation.) Within this last step, it is equally important to initiate evaluation measures to ensure that desired results are achieved. (This was done in the Cape Hatteras sea turtle example, where evaluation of the outcomes resulted in changing the approach. At Point Reyes, improved plover population levels served as measurable indicators of program success.)

These four interrelated steps seek to incorporate current best practices drawn from time-honored, traditional interpretive methodologies, as well as emerging and innovative communications approaches geared toward addressing and helping to resolve specific resource issues. In brief, the goal of this form of problem-solving interpretation is to assist with improving, stabilizing, or resolving human-influenced resource issues and situations through active customized communications. A detailed discussion of each of these four essential steps and additional contributing factors follows.

Websites Referenced

1. http://www.nps.gov/pore/naturescience/birds_snowyplover.htm
2. http://www.nps.gov/getc/naturescience/index.htm
3. http://www.nps.gov/policy/mp2006.pdf
4. http://www.nationalgeographic.com/field/projects/bioblitz.html
   http://www.dlia.org/atbi
   http://atbialliance.org
5. http://www.scienceprogress.org/2008/04/engaging-the-scientific-community-with-the-public

Engaging the Four-Step Resource Issue Communications Process

Utilizing I + A + M + T = RP to Achieve Effective Stewardship Results

The four-step Resource Issue Communications Formula is akin to the highly successful Interpretive Equation. While the formula places primary emphasis on defining resource issues and situations in order to engender effective solutions, it is similar to the interpretive equation in that it recognizes the importance of knowing and understanding the target audience and using appropriate interpretive techniques and methods for reaching them.

The Interpretive Equation was developed by NPS interpreters as a training and guidance tool. The equation consists of assuring that the interpreter has sufficient Knowledge of the Resource (KR), combined with Knowledge of the Audience (KA), combined with Appropriate Techniques (AT) to achieve a successful Interpretive Outcomes or Opportunities (IO). In formulaic shorthand, the Interpretive Equation is (KR + KA) x AT = IO.

> It is important that the individual nature and scope of an issue be identified before attempting to proceed with its resolution.

The Resource Issue Communications Formula adds several important additional ingredients, including defining the issue and the affiliated human dimension factors related to the situation, as well as establishing the appropriate message that needs to be conveyed to achieve successful stewardship results. The rest of the formula remains similar, with recognition of the importance of selecting the most appropriate interpretive techniques or approaches to effectively reach the desired target audiences (with the final outcomes being resource protection). Thus the Resource Issue Communications Formula consists of identifying the Issue, Audience, Message, and Technique, in order to achieve Resource Protection. In academic shorthand it is I + A + M + T = RP.

Following are the four steps of the resource issue communications process in expanded detail, with explanations of the sub-activities necessary to achieve successful stewardship results and outcomes.

Step 1. Ask "What is the issue, and to what degree do humans play a role?"
Identifying critical resource issues starts with an initial determination of resource situations or problems, generally through careful science-based study by resource specialists and managers. Within the National Park Service, each park has a resource stewardship plan, general management plan, or other documentation that identifies desired future conditions as well as known resource problems and needs.

The first step is to clearly determine the issue to be addressed (based on legitimate needs for park management to resolve or address such issues) and the human factors affiliated with that issue. Current NPS guidance documents identify the following as prominent broad-scale critical resource topics:

Dark Night Sky
Natural Sounds
Ocean Stewardship
Climate Change
Invasive Species
Natural Role of Fire
Sacred Sites of Traditionally Associated Groups
Archeological Resource Protection
Cultural Landscapes Restoration

Additional, more site-specific examples include:

Exotic Plant and Animal Management Activities
Endangered Species Protection Initiatives
Wild and Scenic River Stewardship Activities
Prairie Habitat Maintenance Programs
Wildlife Habituation and Mitigation Programs
Bear Management Activities
Native Animal Reintroduction Initiatives
Native Plant Revegetation Programs
Water Quality Monitoring and Mitigation Activities
Air Quality Initiatives
Wildlife Population Dynamics Management
Erosion of Archeological Sites on Shorelines
Traditional Cultural Uses for Preserved Landscapes
Oil and Gas Drilling
Shoreline Erosion
Disturbed Lands

Specific issues within these categories differ from area to area, such as the issues at Cape Hatteras, Point Reyes, and Gettysburg. Some adverse influences may have been caused by inappropriate past management practices (such as predator reduction programs, improper preservation techniques for historic features, excessive natural fire suppression, or jetty construction adjacent to shorelines). Others issues are caused by a growing number of external factors. It is important that the individual nature and scope of an issue be identified before attempting to proceed with its resolution. Communicating and working in tandem with scientists and resource management specialists, therefore, is crucial at this juncture.

Many critical resource issues have a local focus. Wildlife roadkill, unique habitat restoration needs, looting of cultural sites, flooding of historic structures, and negative human-wildlife situations are but a few examples. At the other end of the spectrum are broad-scale issues such as climate change that affect virtually every park.

NATIONAL PARK SERVICE

Cape Hatteras National Seashore

Within this initial step it is important to determine the degree of human involvement related to both the source of the problem and potential communications-based solutions or improvements. The Cape Hatteras and Point Reyes examples represent issues that are essentially completely generated by humans and resolvable by identifiable user groups. The Gettysburg cultural landscape example represents more indirect issues that generally do not require specific human behavioral change—resource condition improvements can be carried out primarily by management but still benefit significantly from improved public understanding. Because people can be both the cause and the solution for resource management issues, communications will always be a highly preferred management option.

Fully identifying an issue and the degree of associated human involvement enables the development of subsequent steps for seeking resolution through effective communications. By doing so, interpreters can more readily craft appropriate messages and communications products that help affect necessary improvements in understanding or stewardship activities, better identify preferred target audiences capable of making a difference, and more readily determine the most effective communications approaches, tools, and techniques to accomplish the tasks at hand.

Step 2. Determine "What are the key audiences that need to be reached with the message?"

When addressing resource protection issues, the presentation or method of delivery may need to be targeted to specific audiences or user groups to achieve desired results. For example, broad-scale issues such as climate change require getting the message out to large, diversified audiences. On the other hand, specific local issues may benefit from reaching a relatively small target audience that can resolve the issue by modifying behavior locally.

As with all other forms of interpretation, programs and presentations addressing critical resource issues need to clearly identify the desired outcomes. These considerations can be accomplished in part by establishing broad mission goals as well as more refined and measurable program objectives.

Likewise, individual resource protection issue presentations may need to reach both supporters and non-supporters. In seeking real solutions, the most appropriate target audience should not be missed by unwittingly delivering the message solely to a more convenient or traditional audience (as was exemplified in the Gettysburg tree-cutting example).

Step 3. Determine "What is the specific resource protection message that needs to be conveyed to improve or resolve the issue?"

As noted earlier, resolution of different issues requires different levels of acceptance, understanding, or response from the public. Some resource issues may need only a general understanding of or passive support for management actions. Other issues, however, may require significant changes in attitude or stewardship actions by specific individuals or user groups and sometimes the linking of local issues with global ones. The resource protection message for the Cape Hatteras sea turtle issue was, "Nesting turtles need people to stay away from them and their nests." The resource protection message at Kings Mountain is, "People can volunteer to participate in metal detecting activities in appropriate, non-destructive ways that help preserve cultural resources." Each situation requires different levels of public response or civic engagement.

By determining the level of action needed to help resolve an issue, the field manager can also determine the objectives of the message. Here are three examples with increasing degrees of public involvement:

(a) Issues that Would Benefit from Enhanced General Understanding

While some resource issues are relatively benign, others are more controversial because of their perceived deviation from traditional or previously accepted resource management practices. Examples include allowing lightning-caused fires to burn under appropriate conditions in certain wilderness areas rather than being automatically suppressed, or the policy of removing aesthetically attractive but biologically detrimental non-native plant or animal species from park landscapes. Resource management activities surrounding such issues often need varying degrees of explanation to be understood and accepted by the public. Otherwise, such practices may be seen as contradictory to the established purposes of the park (and may undermine public and possibly even legislative support). General articles, web postings, civic presentations, posters, press releases, or fact sheets may be appropriate, and sufficient, for these situations. It is important that such offerings be accurate, science-based, and of interest to the recipients.

(b) Issues that Would Benefit from Significant Changes in Widespread Public Opinions or Misperceptions
Some resource issue solutions may run counter to popular or widely accepted public opinion. Tree cutting at Gettysburg, for instance, seems strange at a time when forests are being depleted as a result of development. Overpopulation of large game (e.g., white-tailed deer) in some parks and suggested management solutions can generate similar degrees of public interest and reaction. Interpretive programs and activities addressing such controversial issues must go beyond developing understanding and appreciation of the resource. Messages must also address the complexity of the issues affecting the resource and the need to select the most-desired alternatives for resolving specific critical resource problems.

Interpretive activities for such situations need to foster an understanding of resource management activities and, if necessary, promote changes in perceptions to broaden support for selecting specific resource management actions over others. The greater the public misunderstanding or confusion, the more time is needed to improve understanding and gain support.

(c) Issues that Would Benefit from Direct Changes in Individual Stewardship Behavior
A number of resource issues require specified human activity change, in addition to improved understanding, to be successfully resolved. Examples include closing certain hiking or camping areas to reduce human-bear encounters or shutting down popular sections of a trail to reduce erosion. At Cape Hatteras and Point Reyes, humans simply needed to change their behaviors voluntarily during limited seasons to solve the problem. The Leave No Trace program provides a set of guidelines for park users when they encounter natural or cultural resources. The National Park Service, along with other federal and local agencies, promotes the Leave No Trace program as an educational tool towards the protection of our national lands. Great Basin National Park and Lake Clark National Park and Preserve are two examples of national parks that use Leave No Trace education as an interpretive tool for the preservation of natural and cultural resources.

Some broad-scale environmental issues, such as air quality and water quality, may ultimately require the mitigation of certain adverse actions outside park boundaries. Objectives for developing messages for such interpretive responses should identify the desired outcomes up front. Presentations should be engaging, science-based, and factual and avoid being didactic and negative.

Step 4. Determine "What is the most appropriate communications approach for delivering the message?"

All too often, resource issue–focused interpretive programs have failed or been ineffective because inappropriate communications approaches, techniques, or tools were used. For this reason, a range of possibilities should be surveyed before making the final choice. A mix-and-match approach that uses several communications approaches simultaneously may be most effective. During program development, messages and delivery systems need to be pilot-tested with intended audience members to ensure their effectiveness.

Muir Woods National Monument

Previous studies have identified the following prominent communications tools, techniques, and methods:

live talks	movies	TV
brochures	maps	periodicals
school programs	signs	roving staff in backcountry
guidebooks	wayside panels	posters
internet	personnel at public meetings	displays at visitor centers
power point slide shows	radio	press releases

It would be easy to expand this list with additional options, especially with the plethora of emerging communications technologies today. And indeed, innovation is encouraged. The key is to match the selected communications approach or technique with access to, and interest by, the desired target audience. At Cape Hatteras, well-intended initial efforts used traditional, established interpretive approaches but ended up without achieving positive results. The follow-up innovative approach was more successful than previous attempts at reaching the desired audience (local residents), who were needed to resolve this particular resource protection issue.

In the Pacific West Region, an initiative to encourage the use of "weed-free feed" by horse owners who use equestrian trails in parks recognized that simply distributing brochures at park visitor centers would only result in limited success, since many riders do not come to the visitor center. Methods that reach horse owners more directly are therefore constantly being investigated. Similarly, "climber coffees" at Yosemite were instrumental in reaching certain visitor groups that seldom were reached through or receptive to typical visitor communications methods.

Site stewardship programs throughout the federal government encourage the public to become personally invested in preserving archeological resources and, by extension, all cultural resources. Hands-on learning, citizen-science programming, special events, and exhibits are among the many possibilities for applying appropriate communications approaches and methods to engender (as noted in the Developing and Implementing Archeological Site Stewardship Programs 2007 technical bulletin).[1]

Evaluation is an equally important ingredient to include within this step. The Interpretation and Education Evaluation Summit of 2006 noted, "The NPS should not assume a 'one size fits all' approach. Evaluation strategies should be designed to meet the needs of the stakeholders." Evaluation helps us understand what works, what does not, why, and how to increase the effectiveness of our outreach efforts for the purposes of resource protection and preservation.

Since resource issue interpretation uses a combination of traditional techniques and current problem-solving considerations, evaluation processes set up for either of these approaches can be used. Critical issue evaluation should consider such factors as relevance of the message to the audience (potentially detectable by observable improvements in public attitudes) or, where appropriate, positive measurable changes in resource-related behavior.

Serious consideration should be given to evaluating "resource condition" as an additional form of measuring interpretive success. At Muir Woods National Monument, social scientists working with the NPS Natural Sounds Program monitored adverse human background noise levels both before and after implementing experimental interpretive products geared toward informing visitors about the values of natural sounds and natural quiet. When the interpretive products were in place, statistically measurable improvements in natural sound quality occurred. When the experimental interpretive products were removed, sound quality levels regressed. In much the same way, human-bear conflicts at Yosemite National Park have been reduced as a result of developing customized interpretive resource protection messages and products.[2]

Websites Referenced

1. http://www.nps.gov/archeology/pubs/techBr/tch22.htm
2. http://www.nature.nps.gov/ParkScience/index.cfm?ArticleID=346

Integrating Other Important Ingredients to Achieve Positive Outcomes

Use Current State-of-the-Art Practices

Using communications to promote resource appreciation and understanding, as well as to improve or resolve critical issues and problems, is both an art and a science. A number of complementary ingredients can help ensure that the recommended measures lead to positive results.

The National Association for Interpretation provides a wide variety of publications, training resources, and on-line materials that provide state-of-the art guidance and advice for successful interpretation. Similarly, the NPS Interpretive Process Model offers sound foundational guidance for developing effective interpretive products and services that offer opportunities for audiences to make emotional and intellectual connections to the meanings of the resource.[1]

> When translating scientific or technical information, it is important to integrate appropriate personal and emotional ingredients into the message when possible.

When translating scientific or technical information into an interpretive communications product, it is important to integrate appropriate personal and emotional ingredients into the message when possible. Social science and related media studies have verified that when communicating with the public, emotion commonly trumps facts in most science-based discussions or presentations.[2]

With this consideration in mind, with the multitude of ongoing and emerging resource threats, now more than ever is the time for interpreters to use their powerful skills for making subjects meaningful and relevant in order to reignite passion for the tangible, intangible, and inspirational values of critical resources. Bringing passion to a subject can also bring about understanding, empathy, and concern.

Traditional time-honored interpretive techniques can shine in this regard. For example, interpreters are capable of bringing out the awe and splendor of the night sky, the impressive size and distance of distant stars and galaxies, the magnitude of space, the miracle of a "living" planet Earth when seen from space. They can also remind us of Earth's visible systems and patterns. Similarly, reconnecting visitors with the awesomeness of natural soundscapes can bring comprehension, as well as a call to action. The spine-chilling howls of a wolf that break the deep quiet of a starry night, the muffled but permeating hoot-hoot-hoot of an owl, the hushed voices and the crackling of a cheerful campfire, and a volley of rifle fire at a Civil War site are elemental and memorable moments that last a lifetime.

Develop a Thematic Statement or Slogan

A theme—a central idea around which a program revolves and from which it evolves—is an effective way to instill or provoke interest in a subject. As recommended within the NPS Interpretive Process Model, a theme is the main idea or unifying thread that weaves continuously through an interpretive program. Themes can draw relationships from other subject areas, similar to the use of parables or analogies, to fill out a story and make it more interesting. Themes can also be used as mechanisms for building relationships between the audience and the subject.

Enos Mills

For the Point Reyes western snowy plover issue, a theme might be the broad workings of wildlife ecology in a national park setting or how "home is where the habitat is." When the Heartland Inventory and Monitoring Network developed its education and outreach communications plan, it selected the theme that it "protects the habitat of our heritage" to describe its overarching role with both natural and cultural sites. Similarly, the NPS Natural Resource Office of Education and Outreach adopted the slogan that its mission supports "using communications to protect our natural heritage."[3]

Assure Relevancy and Accuracy

As stated earlier, regardless of the program or medium selected, the delivery needs to be relevant and meaningful to the targeted audience to be effective. Most resource issues are initially recognized and described by resource scientists or others with advanced training or credentials. However, frequently the resource protection message's target audience includes individuals who will not be familiar with specific scientific or academic terms or complex analytical assessments. Prominent Rocky Mountain naturalist Enos Mills noted in Adventures of a Nature Guide (1920), "The nature guide is at his best when he discusses facts so that they appeal to the imagination and to the reason, give flesh and blood to cold facts, and make life stories of inanimate objects."

The key to resolving this matter is finding ways to combine current scientific findings with effective audience-oriented communication techniques. For example, the message on the successful Cape Hatteras postcards contained the following science-based yet compelling interpretive text:

> On a summer night, a 300-pound loggerhead sea turtle hauls herself onto the beach to nest as her ancestors have done for thousands of years. Any interference can cause this threatened animal to return to the water without laying her eggs. Her young hatchlings are needed to rebuild the greatly depleted population. If you see a sea turtle at night crawling from the surf: Do not approach her. Keep voices down and lights out. Leave her undisturbed. Report sightings to a park ranger.

It is equally paramount to ensure that information presented is accurate, current, and verifiable and matches organizational policies and guidelines. For federal employees, the Information Quality Act (Section 515 of Public Law 106-554) places strict guidelines on federal government scientific information dissemination, often requiring peer review and other quality assurances. At times interpretive materials can be considered an official means of disseminating park policy or science-based management determinations. Therefore, it is critical that the contents of such information be appropriately reviewed and approved in advance of distribution, particularly when the topic is complex or controversial. Because scientific findings and policy determinations are often subject to revisions and modifications, it is equally important to present the most recent agency position or determination in any presentation.[4]

Speak and Write for Target Audiences

Scientific writing by design requires extensive verification of facts and documentation of findings. Scientific writing, however, can be very hard to follow. Many scientific reports are so technical in nature and laced with jargon that they can only be deciphered by fellow specialists. Examples of good popular treatments of various resource topics can be found in films and publications produced by organizations like the National Geographic Society, History Channel, Archaeology Channel, Smithsonian Institution, and Audubon Society. The key is clarity, simplicity, and use of common language and analogies. Noted naturalist John Muir left us with the following observation: "In drying plants, botanists often dry themselves. Dry words and dry facts will not fire hearts."

According to the U.S. Census Bureau, the American population is growing more ethnically and racially diverse, with nearly a quarter of the citizens identifying themselves as Black, Hispanic, Asian and Pacific Islander, or American Indian. By 2045, ethnic minority groups are expected to make up almost half the population. Yet, minorities are frequently underrepresented in visitor populations at national parks and other similar venues. Research indicates cultural differences in outdoor use, such as Hispanic Americans visiting parks in larger groups with extended families. Research also indicates that visitors to parks with cultural themes expect to recognize something of themselves in what they see, be it a discussion of an ethnic group's particular story in America, everyday life, or artifacts they recognize from personal experience. Often, the relationships between natural and cultural resources are important keys to the story. Interpreters can use human dimensions data to target the needs and desires of existing and potential visitors to encourage communication with more diverse stakeholders.

Interpretation can help maintain interest and increase visitation at parks and other areas, but interpreters can also use current technology, such as websites and social networking sites, to reach

Morristown National Historical Park

beyond the parks to communicate with youth and adults. Podcasts offer another medium with great potential. Interpretation can emphasize potential visitor self-interests—physical and emotional health and other quality of life issues—through effective communication of the benefits of outdoor activities.

Relate to the Area's Purpose or Mission, Combine Resource Themes Where Appropriate

At park areas that have been set aside primarily for their outstanding natural features, it is relatively easy to incorporate resource protection messages in interpretive programming. However, it can be challenging to address a resource protection issue that is not one of the more obvious site themes. For example, concerns about invasive species on the surface lands of a cave park may require some creative messaging to reassure the public that the park story is more complex than it may seem at first glance.

In park areas set aside primarily for their cultural features, modern-day resource concerns can often be correlated with past human activities. Many cultural resource areas have stories that are historically linked to significant natural features, processes, or events. Thomas Edison and George Washington Carver both experimented with natural plant materials to produce new goods and products. Alexander Graham Bell, Guglielmo Marconi, and the Wright brothers all took advantage of natural features to enhance their experimentation. Thomas Jefferson was a superb naturalist. Ben Franklin was keenly aware of natural systems (identifying the Gulf Stream among other things). Lewis and Clark were the nation's first inventory and monitoring team, and their records contributed greatly to the ethnographic description of Native American tribes in the West.

Because many cultural resource sites contain significant amounts of "protected landscapes," it is sometimes tempting to overlook the historical significance of these areas and talk instead about current resource issues independently. Generally, however, a stronger message can be delivered by linking past activities with current situations.

For example, at Morristown National Historical Park, managing excessive deer populations is a current natural resource issue; when George Washington and the Continental Army camped there during the winter of 1779, however, this situation was reversed. The deer population was smaller then, not because of over harvesting, but more so because of the lack of prime habitat due to extensive farming and land clearing. A powerful and interesting story lies within these differences. Similarly, visitors may enter wilderness areas with the misperception that humans never lived in or used these areas. The archeological record often offers an interesting way to interpret human-land interactions over thousands of years. Likewise, the historic uses and capture of natural sources of energy may be a topic that helps cultural sites integrate with current climate change discussions.

Cultural considerations deserve recognition when interpreting natural resource issues. They may well be the connection needed to make a presentation more relevant or interesting to the intended audience.

Develop a Resource Condition and Stewardship Communications Matrix

Developing a critical resource issue communications "matrix" is a form of organization that can aid significantly in preparing and delivering resource issue messages (see matrix example on page 73). A matrix of this sort does not need to be complex to make the effort successful but should address major considerations. All major NPS Natural Resource Preservation Program projects that exceed specified dollar levels (e.g. exceed $100,000) require that an "Interpretive Component" activity, approach, or action plan accompany the project. Guidelines ask that preparers fill in a matrix that incorporates the following considerations:

- articulation of the issue;
- associated human dimension factors;
- solution-based message;
- target audience;
- interpretive approach or techniques;
- interpretive contact who will be working in partnership with the resource issue specialist on this particular project;
- evaluation strategies;
- timetable; and
- proposed budget.[5]

Include Other Communicators

Interpreters can augment the effectiveness of critical resource issue communications by collaborating with other communicators. The Interpretation and Education Renaissance Action Plan (National Park Service, 2006) calls for interpreters to serve as catalysts in this regard by using their extensive communications skills and knowledge to inform and empower other communicators, including volunteers, concessioners, educators, and partners. It is equally important to cross-link with other NPS employees who are involved in public contact and communications. These groups include public affairs personnel, law enforcement rangers, maintenance employees, and resource management specialists. Each of these communication sources provides additional opportunities for directing resource protection messages to appropriate audiences.

Journal of Interpretation Research

Providing other organizations and appropriate partners with information and materials that will enable them to customize presentations for their own audiences can help to spread the message. The media, if appropriately engaged, can also play a beneficial role in promoting public comprehension and understanding of stewardship needs. Agency public affairs specialists can be particularly helpful with these efforts and should be brought into the process when and where appropriate.

It is also important to consider the importance of customizing the packaging of messages and delivery style for other messengers. For example, law enforcement rangers are often the park's most visible line of defense in protecting its resources. They routinely meet scores of park visitors and stakeholders, engaging in multiple, brief personal contacts throughout the day. Their public relations skills are considered paramount ingredients to their identity. It has been found that the more enforcement personnel know about the resources they are protecting, the better off they are at doing their jobs. Colorado State University Professor George Wallace verified this concept by studying the benefits of using the "authority of the resource" rather than the "authority of regulations" when communicating and/or enforcing resource protection infractions. Wallace's studies showed that resource stewardship compliance increased when enforcement personnel cited the importance of the resource, rather than merely identifying rules and regulations.[6]

There are advantages to supporting protection rangers and other public contact communicators (such as maintenance personnel, field resource management workers, fee collectors, information station staff, and concessionaires) with synthesized and/or pre-packaged resource issue "talking points" or similar summaries of important stewardship messages. With this method, individuals with only limited time to explain a particular issue have the knowledge to summarize main points. Condensed support material can also assist the "communicator" in guiding visitors toward finding additional information on their own (e.g., park websites, information displays at visitor centers, and scheduled presentations by subject experts).

Involve Citizens and Partners When and Wherever Possible

Resource stewardship programs and activities that directly involve the public can have powerful and lasting effects. Many parks have enlisted the help of volunteers to become "Weed Warriors" to help with the removal of non-native invasive plant species. Rocky Mountain National Park has a volunteer "Bighorn Brigade" that helps with resource management concerns relating to bighorn sheep and a volunteer "Bugle Corps" that assists with traffic control and public information services during the elk rut. Volunteer programs at Lowell and Steamtown involve volunteers in the upkeep of historic machinery. The Geoscientists-in-the-Parks program connects subject matter professionals with volunteer opportunities in parks. The Student Conservation Association has placed thousands of individuals in parks to perform resource stewardship activities. The Park Flight program involves Americans as well as citizens from other countries in bird conservation, since migratory flyways and related stewardship needs cross international boundaries. Several parks have volunteer on-site stewardship programs to monitor archeological sites.[7]

Offering and promoting environmental education programs has been a long-standing mission of the National Park Service. Residential environmental education centers at Everglades National Park, Cape Cod National Seashore, and many other parks have served hundreds of thousands of students. Resource stewardship and protection messages are routinely a part of these programs. Partnering with schools can help build long-term stewardship ethics among their students, along with support for park values and active management to ensure resource protection. One key to success is to assure that curriculum materials prepared by the host organization match with teaching requirements. When teachers are given something that matches with and helps reduce their workload, there is greater buy in.

Electronic educational programs can also reach the American population in positive and creative ways. The Service-wide Web Ranger program and the web-based Views of the National Parks program offer innovative and interactive ways for individuals to learn more about critical resource topics. Night sky, natural sound, ocean stewardship, climate change, and other critical resource topics are presented by these programs.[8]

The NPS Research Learning Center network is committed to enhancing connections with educational programs related to resource topics and issues in parks. For example, the Appalachian Highlands Science and Learning Center in Great Smoky Mountains National Park has developed an outstanding program where students participate in realistic inventory and monitoring activities. One particularly effective exercise focuses on ozone monitoring, with students collecting field data and analyzing bio-indicators (e.g., spotting patterns in leaves) to determine ozone trends.[9]

The "Leave No Child Inside" initiative offers hope that American society will see value in reconnecting with the world outside their door. Affiliated with that is hope for an increase in citizen awareness of resource stewardship needs and obligations.[10] Well-crafted resource stewardship information can be picked up and utilized mutually by a variety of sources, including scouting organizations and religious groups (such as the growing environmental evangelical movement,[11] as well as the physical and mental health communities (e.g., those affiliated with First Lady Michelle Obama's "Let's Move" campaign).[12]

Balance Perspectives

Developing a well-balanced perspective is essential to success. Within the resource issue interpretation and education guidelines, NPS Management Policies states that "park managers are increasingly called upon to make difficult resource decisions, some of which may be highly controversial. Interpretive and educational programs can build public understanding of, and support for, such decisions and initiatives, and for the NPS mission in general. Therefore, parks should in balanced and appropriate ways, thoroughly integrate resource issues and initiatives of local and Service-wide importance into their interpretive and educational programs" (NPS Management Policies 7.5.3). The NPS Interpretive Development Program also recognizes the importance of incorporating multiple perspectives within interpretive presentations.[13]

In this regard, it is important that the interpreter serve as a "credible voice" when discussing resource issues with the public. National Park Service employees enjoy an extremely high degree of trust by the public. It is important to keep that trust intact by not overly embellishing or sensationalizing issues and concerns that affect park resources. On the other hand, it is appropriate and necessary to present serious resource protection issues and concerns openly and sincerely to the public.

Avoid Thinking that "One Size Can Fit All"

Resource protection issues—and parks—may seem similar, but in most cases it is important to consider the customization of both the message as well as the technique for addressing any given critical resource issue. With all the variables that contribute to a resource issue, it makes sense to look at all the variables that could lead to its understanding and/or resolution. Hence, it is best not to borrow exclusively from products or materials prepared for another similar issue or location but to customize or augment the presentation to cover the unique factors of the problem and situation at hand.

There is value to having attractive, compelling, well-designed promotional materials or presentations for any outreach effort. There is additional benefit when localized issues can be identified and linked to broad-scale ones. With the climate change issue, for example, it is beneficial to have both national and local examples and messages. The task is to allow room, whenever and wherever possible, for linking both broad-scale and localized information.[14]

Market the Message Effectively and Appropriately

Some critical resource issues require only small, relatively simple solutions, while others require large-scale solutions. For example, some local issues, such as remediating erosion caused by cross-cutting on a seldom-used trail, may only need a few people to change their ways. Climate change, on the other hand, is a large-scale matter that requires the involvement of whole societies. Social scientists have found that regardless of the issue, audiences are more receptive when positive alternatives and reasonable explanations are offered to them for any given situation. Thus, when marketing or promoting a resource stewardship message, it is important to take into consideration the audience's interests, understandings, and beliefs. Similarly, if the interpretive product fails to reach a sufficient quantity of recipients necessary to satisfactorily address the resource issue, the effort may appear outwardly successful (due to the attractiveness of the product or enthusiasm of the presenter) but may be unsuccessful in its measurable results. Effectively reaching an appropriate quantity of recipients is, thus, an important factor.

Consider, for example, the Smokey Bear campaign. While it may be important to modify and update Smokey's message to help explain the values of prescribed burning, the original Smokey campaign to "engage a wide range of citizens to be careful about starting unintended forested fires" has been clearly successful. Similarly, the "Don't Mess with Texas" anti-littering campaign indirectly used the premise that if you're a Texan, you don't want anyone messing with your state by littering and, moreover, if you're not a Texan, you don't want a Texan mad at you for littering! This program has also shown measurable success. But to be fully successful, both campaigns needed to reach (and get buy-in from) a critical mass of recipients.

Smokey Bear

Costly programs that only get occasional laudatory feedback from relatively small numbers of recipients and fail to reach the necessary critical mass are not only inappropriate expenditures of funds but also may give false impressions that either the communications solution is working or that communications programs in general are an ineffective management tool (because results were not achieved). Similarly, an overly exuberant presenter may make a program or product appear successful, getting high acclaim from those limited recipients who are fortunate enough to receive the "full dose" of their enthusiasm. But if doing so hampers the appropriate distribution of the message to the wider audience needed to achieve effective results, then this sort of activity can be counterproductive. To remedy this, evaluation of desired results must be built into the effort throughout the process. By using the four-step process in reverse order as an evaluation procedure tool, desired results can be measured and effective outcomes rated.

Formative evaluation is another method whereby—prior to developing the final product—prototypes are tested, market research is conducted, and social science activities (e.g., surveys or focus groups) are used to determine pre-established attitudes and beliefs. By taking formative evaluation steps at the beginning to ensure that the preferred audience has been selected and the intended message can be appropriately received, there is greater assurance that the effort will be successful. The ultimate measure is verifiable improvements in resource condition (e.g., reduced inappropriate noise levels, lower numbers of human-bear encounters, reduced archaeological disturbance, reduced spread of invasive species) when such measurements are possible.[15]

Evaluation can at times be expensive or time consuming. When limited funds or resources are available, a variety of alternatives still exist. If surveys are difficult to get approval for, focus groups or audience observation can be a reasonable alternative. By using a project management–style approach, with objectives stated at the beginning and checks and re-checks made along the way, effective results can be enhanced (or, conversely, non-successes identified and used as "lessons learned" for future improvements).[16] Interpreters also can learn from the results of previous evaluation. For example, formative evaluation has been used to identify that better results can be achieved from an electronic media presentation that develops a promotional DVD to serve as a teaser for the product (including a web link to the full product) rather than distributing the entire product on a DVD. This approach was drawn from studies conducted by the Colorado State University Department of Journalism and Technical Communications when evaluating the effectiveness of the message and delivery mechanisms of an alcohol awareness education and outreach program for college students.[17]

In summary, scientists and resource managers can supply important findings and data surrounding a critical resource issue. They can also help facilitate the development of appropriate messages that will help communicate desired outcomes and future conditions. What interpretive professionals can offer is a capacity for developing emotional and intellectual connections between the resource, the issue, and the audience, along with additional advanced communications techniques and methods. Thus, by working as a team and by following the steps necessary to assure that appropriate communications approaches are selected, desired message crafted, preferred audience determined, and appropriate evaluation procedures integrated throughout the process, the chances for success are greatly elevated. Similarly, effective marketing is an important ingredient to assure that all of the good work done via this process is indeed made available to the desired audiences. This is as relevant today as it was over 100 years ago, when parks were cooperatively "defended by poets." Passion can indeed enhance articulation and promote comprehension.

Serve as a "Voice for the Resource"

NPS Management Policies clearly recognizes the need for protecting park resources as a paramount requirement:

> The Secretary has an absolute duty, which is not to be compromised, to fulfill the mandate of the 1916 Act to take whatever actions and seek whatever relief as will safeguard the units of the national park system. (2006 NPS Management Policies 1.4.2)

The 1916 Organic Act underscores the obligation of park management to protect resources as the highest priority—clearly delineating the need for the National Park Service to serve as a protector of and voice for the resource. To this end, interpretation can be a powerful and highly desired management tool. As stated earlier, when critical resource situations require action, the park manager can address such problems with a spectrum of tools. Depending on the severity of the issue, these options may range from closing an area to the public (generally used only under extreme conditions), to increasing enforcement efforts (which can be potentially costly or adversarial), to developing and implementing targeted interpretive communications activities (designed to be as user friendly as possible), or ultimately seeking legislative or regulatory support (again, potentially complex, lengthy, and requiring much overhead support). Communications as a solution often will be a highly preferred option—one that can be used alone or as a complement to whatever additional alternative is selected.[18]

To successfully address public perceptions and speak for imperiled park resources, a well-coordinated interpretive outreach effort is important. In the examples given throughout this publication, park staff used sound science and proven methods of public outreach to achieve their goals.

The park visitor interacts with park resources in a number of ways. One is directly with the landscape and features of the park. Another is with the educational materials and exhibits in the park. Yet another is with interpreters and other park employees who are involved with public contact. In addition, the park visitor usually has only a limited amount of time—from a few hours to a few days at the most—to spend in a park. Thus, the opportunity to affect the stewardship interests of visitors is restricted and must be carefully planned to be effective. Often, a park's entire staff, not just resource managers and interpreters, must join together to reach the goal.

A growing number of resource issues have origins outside park boundaries, thus creating potential audiences that may be separate or different from traditional park visitors. Therefore interpretive efforts must be designed with the understanding that there may be only limited opportunities for direct contact with these audiences.

Park staff members are often the primary spokespeople for safeguarding the park, and they have a special mission to do so as outlined in a park's enabling legislation or other regulations or policy guidelines. The mission of park interpreters may seem simple—to protect the park through promoting understanding and appreciation—but successfully doing so today often requires telling a much more convincing and compelling story to the public, one that uses professional, well-coordinated, well-articulated, and appropriately targeted presentations.

In doing this important work, interpretive professionals help lead the way toward promoting enduring, comprehensive, and critical stewardship of our nation's natural and cultural heritage, located within its parks and protected areas.

Websites Referenced

1. http://www.nps.gov/idp/interp/101/processmodel.pdf
2. http://www.eci.ox.ac.uk/research/climate/downloads/tippingpoint/.../boykoff.pdf
3. http://science.nature.nps.gov/im/units/htln
4. http://www.whitehouse.gov/sites/default/files/omb/memoranda/fy2005/m05-03.pdf
5. http://www.nature.nps.gov/educationoutreach/interpretivesolutions
6. http://www.interpnet.com/JIR/archive.htm
7. http://www.nature.nps.gov/climatechange/citizenscience.cfm
   http://www.nature.nps.gov/climatechange/internshipsresearch.cfm
8. http://www.webrangers.us/activities/darksky
   http://www.nature.nps.gov/climatechange/internshipsresearch.cfm
   http://www.nature.nps.gov/views/index.cfm
9. http://www.nature.nps.gov/learningcenters
10. http://www.govtrack.us › Congress › Legislation

11. http://www.washingtonpost.com
12. http://www.letsmove.gov/getactive.php
13. http://www.nps.gov/idp/interp
14. http://science.nature.nps.gov/im/units/htln/edoutrch.cfm
15. http://www.today.colostate.edu/story.aspx?id=3449
16. http://www.pmi.org
17. http://www.nature.nps.gov/educationoutreach/interpretivesolutions
18. http://www.nps.gov/legacy/organic-act.htm
    http://www.nps.gov/history/history/online_books/anps/anps_7e.htm
    http://www.nps.gov/policy/MP2006.pdf

Selecting Appropriate Interpretive Approaches for Communicating Resource Solutions

Packaging the Process

It is important to follow the sequence outlined in the four-step process and not jump into selecting an arbitrary or poorly thought-out interpretive approach or technique. Advancing directly to "interpretive technique" happens all too often, frequently resulting in pre-selecting an approach that may not be the most effective means for reaching the audience in need of being reached or in ways that are relevant to them. This often results in an ineffective solution or squandered funds and resources.

Determining the issue, ideal audience, and best message should always come first. Then, a variety of customized interpretive approaches designed to reach target audiences are required to develop effective resource issue messages. For example, traditional guided walks and talks serve certain local audiences and issues extremely well. Mass media presentations, on the other hand, are generally more effective for reaching broad-scale audiences with broad-scale messages.

Individual interpreters at the local level can ensure one-to-one transfer of environmental messages with individual park visitors.

A multilayered approach often brings the best results for helping to resolve significant resource issues. Individual interpreters at the local level can ensure one-to-one transfer of environmental messages with individual park visitors. Regional and central office personnel can establish contact with media outlets, environmental organizations, other government operations, and/or constituency groups and their representatives. Maintenance workers, concession employees, and other in-park staff can offer an additional layer of public contact.

All too often, advancing to a predetermined interpretive product or approach is the norm. Consider the many times when interpreters, as well as managers, immediately conclude that a brochure about the issue should be developed and distributed at the visitor center. Perhaps a brochure is the most effective tool, but in some cases the target audience will neither stop at the visitor center nor read a brochure. The same holds true for websites. Sometimes websites are excellent ways to get the word out, but at other times they may have only limited value in reaching the desired target audience. Mixing and matching of appropriate media with selected target audiences is essential. The following examples of interpretive techniques to address critical natural resource issues were drawn from field surveys conducted in parks and protected areas. Each is reviewed as to its ability to reach specific (or at times different) target audiences:

Traditional Personal Programs
Handouts and Brochures
Fact Sheets and Park Newspapers
Site Bulletins
Resource Message Panels
Resource Message Exhibits
Bulletin Boards
Portable Exhibits
Interactive Personal Electronic Devices
Explorer Kits
CD Audio Packages
TV and other Home-based Contacts
Educational Support Programs and Materials
Teacher, Group Leader Support Products
Video Presentations and Radio Technology
Partnerships and Volunteers
Innovative Customized Programs
Press Releases and Feature Articles
Cooperative Efforts with Mass Media
Web-based Products and Services
New Media Opportunities

Traditional Personal Programs
Special guided walks and talks continue to play a significant role in interpreting critical resource issues. Guided walks may serve as a "controlled" form of access to fragile resource features. Illustrated talks can be effective alternatives to personal contact with sensitive resources (e.g., archeological site "remote presentations" when rare or fragile artifacts are present).

Traditional walks and talks on general park themes can include messages about specific and broad-based environmental concerns. The themes for such programs often center on subjects such as change and interaction and their effects on natural landscapes and related qualities of human existence.

Walks and talks designed to focus on a specific critical resource issue are best performed by experienced interpreters and may require careful monitoring for accuracy. Sometimes these programs are not the most appropriate method for addressing certain issues. For example, they may

Title: MEADOWS MATTER!

Theme: Intensive Care
Meadows are rich dynamic environments that require special protection to remain healthy.

Goal(s): To explain to park visitors meadow formation and dynamics, and to garner support for a successful meadow restoration program.

Program Objective(s): At the conclusion of the program, the viewer participant should:
- be able to define a meadow;
- be able to describe one natural process that couldresult in the creation of a meadow;
- be able to give one reason why such a diversity of organisms occurs in meadows;
- be motivated to walk only on established trails through meadows, ride a bicycle only on paved surfaces, and avoid wet, fragile areas while walking in or near meadows.

Audience: Visitors to Yosemite National Park of all ages, with widely diverse interests and educational backgrounds. Keyed to walkers near meadows.

Technique: This 20-minute program will be part of a 1-hour ranger talk.

Program Description: Problem Issue: Meadows in Yosemite National Park have been subjected to a great deal of human manipulation and impact during the last 100 or more years. As a result, meadow size and species diversity have been reduced.

Solution Message: Reduction and gradual elimination of future human impact and repair of previous damage will allow processes that created and sustained these meadows to prevail again.

Biological Diversity Connection: Meadows provide the basis for many food chains (e.g., grasses-mice-owls; grasses-insects-shrews-coyotes). Meadows are to Yosemite as rain forests are to this planet (e.g., 36% of Yosemite's plant species occur on 3.5% of Yosemite's land).

Outcome Strategy: Most "volunteer" or unauthorized trails in Yosemite Valley meadows will be eliminated. Hikers will be channeled.

not reach the target audience needed to resolve the problem. Furthermore, they may become dull and unappealing if presented with an apparently biased or overly negative and opinionated delivery style.

When used properly, walks and talks can generate overall understanding of resource issues and can be effective in fostering empathy and public support for resource conservation and management activities. Studies have shown that personal contact between visitors and park employees fostered enhanced comprehension of park subject matters and that "live programs" done well served as a sort of memory glue to promote understanding of resource issues on a long-term basis. Thus, traditional live programs can continue to help to foster appreciation, understanding, and protection.

Live interpretive presentations specifically oriented toward resolving resource issues may need to differ from park area to park area. For example, large, highly visited areas may need to have programs designed to reach significant numbers of once-in-a-lifetime visitors. Other areas may need to construct resource issue programs so that they are not repetitive or redundant to the frequently returning visitor.

Live presentations can benefit from a written outline that provides guidance and reminds the presenter to incorporate important messages and related considerations. Outlines should cover a variety of factors including theme, goals, program objectives, audience composition, agency identification, presentation length, resource issue and message identification, method of delivery, and so on. Audience participation, involvement, enjoyment, and interaction are also key considerations. The initial planning for interpretive programs to address meadow damage in Yosemite Valley benefited from using such an outline. A sample of such a presentation is provided on page 55. Practicing iterations of the presentation in front of critical friends or colleagues can help improve the final performance. Careful observations of target audience members can provide feedback to enhance effectiveness.

Handouts and Brochures

Handouts and brochures can be an effective and relatively low-cost means for providing resource issue information to the public. They range from simple, single-message fliers to full-color brochures devoted to major environmental concerns such as air quality or biological diversity. Handouts and brochures can be designed to reach both local and broad-scale audiences.

A key to the successful reception of the message is effective design. If the design is not enticing or inviting, the message may be overlooked or disregarded. To encourage readability, handouts and brochures should strive for a provocative, concise, and yet interesting style.[1]

The National Park Service has developed a series of brochures designed to address specific critical resource issues. These full-color brochures were modeled to complement existing park area folders. The format of these brochures was arranged similar to current news magazines, with boxed text and captioned illustrations that can be read independently at the reader's discretion. A similar design was adopted for general overviews of additional resource topics.[2]

Brochures, however, are sometimes inadvertently used as the sole interpretive product when in fact they may not be the best means for getting the message to the most important target audience. Care should be taken, therefore, to complete the first steps of the four-step resource issue communications process to assure that appropriate messages, appropriate audiences, and appropriate techniques are considered before product development. On the other hand, brochures are a time-honored means for condensing and presenting information and, if well developed and designed, can be an important tool for spreading the message to appropriate audiences.

For example, the NPS Pacific West Region developed a brochure specifically targeted at horse owners. The intent was to distribute this information at locations where horse owners congregate, including commercial feed distribution shops. Similarly, a brochure on the need to be careful to not damage coral reefs while diving or snorkeling was developed for Kaloko Honokohau National Historical Park with the intent of distributing the brochure at dive rental shops and other appropriate locations.

Fact Sheets

Fact sheets can be an effective means for providing simple or condensed versions of critical natural resource information. They are generally only one or two pages in length and contain detailed text printed on one or both sides of the sheet. Occasionally they contain simple but well-designed graphs, charts, diagrams, or appropriate illustrations. Fact sheets benefit from an interesting title that conveys an interpretive theme or message about the information contained in the sheet. Fact sheets can be set up with a unique design or format and lightly illustrated to enhance their appearance. Placing a date of issue somewhere on the fact sheets is advisable so that revised versions can replace older ones as new information becomes available.

Fact sheets at Mount Rainier National Park containing important resource protection information have been created in multiple languages to reach various audiences. Park personnel design layout and text to include articles on various critical resource issues in each edition.[3]

Partner organizations such as the National Park Foundation and park friends groups occasionally produce high-quality compatible resource issue materials. Often these materials are well suited for reaching large, general audiences with specific resource messages.[4]

National Park Foundation website

Park Newspapers

Locally produced but professionally printed park newspapers can be another means of providing pertinent resource issue information to visitors in a succinct manner. Park newspapers are popular and effective because they offer interesting bits of information, trip-planning hints, timetables, etc. They often contain short feature articles. These articles can serve as interesting, concise summaries of critical resource issues or as a means for disseminating information about management or public actions necessary to resolve issues.[5]

Olympic National Park online newsletter

Resource Message Panels

Resource message information panels, initially developed by the Harpers Ferry Interpretive Design Center of the National Park Service, are useful products to address both resource management and safety concerns. They serve as a means for communicating important precautionary or regulatory messages directly on site in a manner that provides preliminary background on the issue as well. Resource message panels can be an effective alternative to traditional regulatory signs that tell people what not to do but not the reasons why.

These screen-printed fiberglass panels, placed at strategic locations such as walkways along ponds or streams or beach-access points, feature a red band and catch-phrase at the top, grayscale graphics and pictographs, and brief text to convey their message. They are much simpler than normal wayside exhibits and, as a result, are much more versatile and less expensive to produce and install (less than $150 per panel in 2010).

Resource message panels are strategically placed along walkways bordering meadows in Yosemite National Park and at public entrances to freshwater ponds at Cape Cod National Seashore. Target audiences are reached directly at the site of the resource, where appropriate behavior and understanding of issues are most critical. The power of this media is that it is tangible, immediate, and experiential, thereby having greater likelihood of an interpretive connection.[6]

In the 1990s illustrated resource message panels began to appear in parks across the country.

Specific Resource Message Exhibits

At times, a specific park resource can also serve as an exemplary feature or model for showing or explaining critical issues or broad-scale environmental concerns. In such cases, exhibits about these features can incorporate messages about major environmental concerns in conjunction with traditional interpretive information. The impact of reaching selected audiences can be quite significant.

A good example is the incorporation of global climate change messages into on-site exhibits at the Columbia Ice Fields in Jasper National Park in Canada. Global climate change is a widespread concern that needs to be brought to the attention of a broad audience. Traditional programs such as campfire lectures and handouts may have only limited appeal to many park visitors who find this subject abstract or vague. On-site exhibits at the ice fields, however, show visitors measurable changes in the immediate setting due to the effects of global climate change, both through on-site markers on the ground showing where the glacier's edge was a few dozen years ago and by photographs of the area showing different alignments of the glacier at the turn of the century. The exhibits at this location convey the message to thousands of visitors annually.[7]

Boot Brush

Bulletin Boards

Bulletin boards can provide visitors with information on critical resource issues, especially those related to seasonal occurrences. They have the advantage of being able to work independently in a broad range of settings—from exceptionally busy visitor areas to extremely isolated ones. People are naturally attracted to bulletin boards because they want to obtain current safety, regulatory, or weather information.

For this reason, bulletin boards can provide a "human" touch. If properly maintained, they convey a feeling that someone in charge has recently left behind an important message but could not be there in person to give it. Bulletin boards are useful for explaining local resource management concerns or activities, such as why prescribed burning is used in some forested areas (Do you see smoke today?) or why specific nonnative plants are actively being removed from the area.

Although bulletin board information must be contained within a relatively limited form, it can still be effective. By using an appropriate agency-identifying design arrangement, bulletin board information can be presented in an attractive and forthright manner. Unfortunately, bulletin boards have the disadvantage of being easy targets for vandalism. Likewise, when left unattended, information can become stale, faded, and dated.

Bulletin boards strategically placed at visitor concentration points can be used to inform visitors about resource conservation issues and provide general information. Bulletin boards in remote settings need regular upkeep, but when properly maintained can provide a personal touch in such settings. Handouts may accompany bulletin boards.

Portable Exhibits

Portable exhibits come in a wide range of sizes and shapes. Many exhibits on the open market already present information on broad-scale environmental issues.

Portable exhibits on critical resource issues can be moved to relevant locations or removed as conditions change and can be used within or outside the park. After the Yellowstone fires, portable exhibits on the natural role of fire in the environment explained to the visiting public the park's position on letting some natural fires burn, problems with excessive suppression activities in the past, and difficulty in dealing with truly catastrophic fire occurrences as a consequence. The temporary portable exhibits were so successful that the park knew that it could use the theme of natural fire in preparing permanent exhibits on "The Role of Fire at Yellowstone" at park visitor concentration points.[8]

Portable exhibits were developed to address the Mississippi Canyon 252 Oil Spill at appropriate locations along the Gulf Coast.[9]

Interactive Electronic Media

Interactive electronic media is a growing means of reaching park users in settings that may or may not offer personal contact. Touchscreen systems can be set up at park information locations, hotels, tourist centers, shopping malls, and the like. Some programs offer printouts of pertinent information.

Interactive, user-friendly personal electronic communications device programs (e.g., cell phones, netbooks, etc.) are becoming ever more popular and can be of service to thousands of users a week. However, it is important to be careful that such devices do not stand between the visitor and the resource: the experience should not be sacrificed for the message. But these products hold great potential if used properly and judiciously.

Explorer Kits and Visitor Engagement Products and Programs

Finding ways to get individuals directly involved in learning about the environment and related concerns is always a challenge. Explorer kits are one means of helping individuals and families find out about their surroundings in an interesting way. Some visitor centers offer free "loaner kits," while others offer them for sale at their non-profit bookstores.

A variation on encouraging involvement is to capitalize on the popular use of personal video cameras. Some parks have been offering individuals free shooting scripts for use while touring through the park. The scripts give interesting information tidbits, optimal vista locations, and commentary the user can read out loud (or dub in later) about park resources and issues.

Many parks have Junior Ranger programs that feature an activity book for participants to complete to obtain recognition. The activity books frequently use critical natural and cultural resource issues for junior ranger exercises. The NPS Intermountain Region's Junior Ranger Night Explorer program, now distributed nationally, teaches appreciation and care of natural lightscapes and how to avoid light pollution.[10]

Compact Disc Audio Products

A specially produced CD may be just what is needed to reach a specific target audience. Road kills of large mammals are a significant problem in many parks, especially in the Canadian Rockies. Kootenay National Park is located amid a heavily used trucking corridor. To form a partnership with truck drivers, the park staff proposed a plan for recording audio CDs with a combination of country and western music and simple but straightforward messages about road kill problems and methods for improving the situation.

Such CDs can be combined with signs, handouts, and other interpretive communication devices to develop a comprehensive program that encourages drivers to participate in getting other drivers to be more careful in the park. As a result of related communication efforts, truck drivers in Canadian national parks in Alberta are signaling oncoming truck drivers about wildlife on roads by turning on their emergency blinker lights and by talking on their CB radios.

Prerecorded audio programs are another means of helping visitors explore and learn about park resources while traveling over park roadways. Resource management messages can be easily incorporated into these programs. Some areas have experimented with this approach for individual nature trails or other park features, sometimes providing electronic listening devices for rent or loan.

Home-Based Contacts

On occasions, low-tech solutions such as sending informational items out by mail can be used to present resource messages to specific audiences, especially those who have actual or potential contact with critical resource features. This approach reaches these individuals with pertinent information so that they might be more supportive of management policies and more aware of the need for changes in stewardship-related behavior.

Mail materials can be sent to preselected postal zones and can be a relatively inexpensive yet effective means of contact. Great care must be taken to ensure that messages sent out in this form are accurate and balanced in perspective, properly present agency policies and mission, are readily understandable, and feature an attractive design. Direct mail programs at Cape Hatteras and Fire Island national seashores have proven to be advantageous in reaching select audiences with critical resource issue information. These direct mail initiatives may sometimes be enhanced through partnership arrangements. Some park areas have found auto insurance companies are willing to incorporate large game road kill (collision hazard) information to clients in fliers sent out along with monthly billing statements. On the other hand, careful consideration must be given to avoid the appearance of promoting "junk mail" or distribution of wasteful paper products.

Local and Regional Subscription TV Services

Community access through subscription television is another means of reaching large numbers of the public on their home turf. Programming on park resources and issues may be of interest to subscription television stations that provide public service time. Some park areas are currently using dedicated community information channels to provide reoccurring information to local users (e.g., through televisions provided in hotel rooms located within or near parks such as Rocky Mountain and Yosemite national parks).[11] Educators involved in studies of National Park Service historic sites can take advantage of the Teaching with Historic Places website.[12]

Educational Curriculum-Based Programs and Resource Materials

Environmental education programs encourage personal understanding of the environment and environmental issues. Lesson plans and other curriculum materials help group leaders to develop appropriate environmental education activities that can be used in or outside the park. Many parks have prepared environmental education materials directly related to specific critical natural resource issues or features. Support materials can be designed for on-site activities (such as groups participating in Yellowstone National Park's Expedition Yellowstone) or for off-site classroom studies of park resources and issues in remote settings.

Teachers have indicated that they appreciate user-friendly materials that are flexible and do not take large amounts of set-up time. Teacher materials at Cape Cod National Seashore are produced in a multifaceted format—brief but comprehensive lesson plans on critical resource issues are accompanied by short videos, student reader sheets (written in a format similar to articles produced for National Geographic World and Ranger Rick magazines), attractively designed but concise fact sheets, and activity plans (for games and other appropriate group activities).[13]

An important key to success is to investigate requirements of national, state, and local teaching standards. When materials prepared by a park match established teaching requirements and ease the teacher's day-to-day teaching burden, there is value to both sides. Being a friendly helper can go far in generating mutual buy-in.

There are also other vehicles for engaging schools in park-related study activities, including Project WET, Project Learning Tree, etc.[14] The National Park Foundation has promoted the Parks as Classrooms campaign, which is designed to encourage schools and parks to connect with each other. Parks are encouraged to develop additional materials for use by teachers or to revise existing materials.[15]

The Views of the National Parks program is an interactive, web-based educational activity program that provides thematic and issue-based park information and teacher information.[16]

A series of electronic field trips co-sponsored by the National Park Foundation and presented at North Cascades National Park and other locations resulted in upwards of 140,000 participants joining in a single "on-line" presentation in 2010.[17]

Support Programs for Instructors

Environmental education program materials can often be used without the on-site assistance of park staff. However, when staff time can be devoted to presenting periodic group leader workshops, the results can be extremely beneficial. If properly motivated and adequately prepared through such workshops, group leaders can reach additional audiences that park staffs might otherwise overlook or lack the staff or time to reach. Teacher workshops at Cabrillo National Monument off the coast of San Diego, California, have provided teachers with hands-on exposure to marine life and an awareness of environmental concerns related to their survival. Individual leader support can be fostered off-site via teleconferencing or computer programs and webinars. Many schools offer teachers release time from their classrooms to attend professional development offerings. Similarly, the Teacher-Ranger-Teacher program allows participating classroom teachers to serve as rangers during the summer with the provision that they integrate their park experiences and learning back into their classroom and to affiliated classrooms and schools to the extent possible.[18]

North Cascades National Park

Video Presentations

Documentary films and video programs on critical resource issues are an additional means of getting the message out to large or diversified audiences. Short, professionally produced video programs can be produced and used at the local level quite effectively.[19]

Channel Islands National Park has used a special live video system to let visitors "experience" sensitive resources, which they cannot see firsthand because the resources are underwater and in restricted areas. The park set up a two-way video camera/intercom system by which the public can actually talk with NPS divers while they inventory and monitor sensitive underwater resources.

Feature-length films are expensive but occasionally within the realm of consideration when produced by appropriate affiliates, such as the National Geographic Society or the Public Broadcasting System (PBS). Quality feature productions can be aired to national audiences. Good presentations on invasive species, climate change, and other critical resource issues are already in circulation.[20] Quality feature-length films are often reproduced and made available as DVDs, further enhancing distribution possibilities. For example, a broadcast-quality video produced by Montana State University for the National Park Service entitled "Invaders of the National Parks" provides viewers with an overview of the invasive species problem within the National Park System and actions that are being taken to resolve these problems.

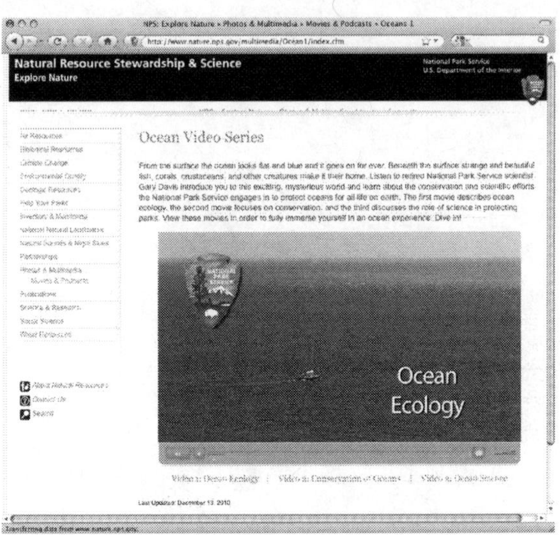

NPS Ocean Video Series online

Films and videos also serve members of the public who are unable to visit parks in person. This is an effective alternate means of understanding and appreciating them. Feature-length professional programs and short, well-produced, locally made programs on resource issues can also be made available for sale through park bookstores or, where appropriate, for loan. Video presentations, which should be captioned, can also be housed on appropriate Internet sites.

The PBS special on national parks produced by Ken Burns included emphasis on resource stewardship and protection needs, devoting an entire segment to George Wright, the prominent natural resource specialists who promoted science-based resource management in the 1930s. Much information about park issues and what is being done to address them was presented in this monumental series.[21]

Broadcast Radio and Transmitted Programs

Radio technology has been used to provide park visitors with short, repeating radio messages 24 hours a day in several park areas. New technology makes modification of messages easier and allows for instantaneous updating of information. Weather information, fire hazards, wildlife problems, and road conditions make these presentations of extreme interest to park users. While most existing systems are short-range, there is potential for expanding broadcasting possibilities (via linking with cellular phone systems) to cover large-scale areas, enabling visitors to obtain park information in remote settings.

Another use of radio is to tie in with public and commercial radio stations to provide periodic park information segments. A series of presentations on various resource topics was created for the PBS "Earth and Sky" series by the NPS Natural Resource Office of Education and Outreach. Many parks are also developing downloadable podcast programs that are becoming increasingly popular.[22]

It is important to keep in mind that such systems and services need continual upkeep and maintenance to stay current and accessible by the intended audience.

Partnership Opportunities, Citizen-Scientist Programs, and Related Volunteer Activities

Creating partnerships for promoting enhanced delivery of resource issue–related messages can result in significant benefits. It has been said that "there are resource managers and resource messengers." Both are needed to address and help resolve critical resource protection problems. Park concession employees, local tour bus operators, and even local hotel and restaurant workers also represent the park and play a big role in presenting its messages to the visiting public. Friends groups and cooperating associations can also play a major role in promoting and disseminating environmental messages. It is important to build bridges with such groups whenever possible.

Some parks are using a novel program to recognize members of the tourist industry by offering periodic awards to outstanding non-park employees in recognition of their superior delivery of key environmental messages to the public. Such awards can consist of a plaque or cash when appropriate. In an attempt to build bridges with the tourism industry, Cape Cod National Seashore and Acadia National Park have developed a means for providing local tour operators a free, comprehensive "Guide's Guide" notebook. These notebooks, available in hard copy and on-line, contain sequential location-by-location information on park resources, interesting facts, figures, stories, and other tour tips. Resource protection messages are an important part of these packages.

Partnership arrangements with nonprofit organizations can help meet needs where operational funds or resources are not readily available. For example, partnership programs with the National Park Foundation have enabled parks to develop and disseminate various environmental education programs and materials, including public distribution of high-quality fact sheets and lesson plans on topics such as climate change and wolf reintroduction.

Nonprofit bookstores operated by friends groups or cooperating associations often serve as a means of generating funds for interpretive programs and activities at parks. Revenues from such sources can be used to fund non-park employee environmental awards, as well as design and production of interpretive materials (e.g., pamphlets, booklets, and video presentations) on critical resource issues. Bookstore operations can help promote environmental messages on the front line as well by promoting environmentally friendly packaging of products and encouraging recycling activities.

Developing partnerships and cooperative activities with concessionaires and other related entities is essential when it comes to ensuring accurate dissemination of environmental messages. Concessioners often are anxious to play a positive role in distributing information about critical resource issues. The Yosemite concession services operation, for example, provides a free color magazine to patrons. Resource issues and public actions that can help in their resolution are routine features of this publication.

It is important to note that without some form of training, review, and approval, concessioners disseminating information about critical resource issues may inadvertently provide inaccurate information or suggest activities that are in direct conflict with park messages. Including them in training and information updating, therefore, is crucial.

Volunteers are another important component of the partnership package. With proper training they can provide live contact with visitors and can assist behind the scenes in a variety of ways. As noted previously, the Geologist-in-Parks Program actively recruits and places individuals with geological expertise in parks. Volunteers at Cape Cod National Seashore help with artifact conservation and cataloguing. A number of parks have developed a "Weed Warrior" volunteer corps to deal with invasive species removal projects.[23]

Building opportunities to involve volunteers in resource conservation activities can be yet another way of establishing partnerships at the personal level. Several park areas have established simple one-day or one-hour projects for interested visitors, such as invasive species weed pulling at certain parks. Junior Ranger programs in some parks also require a helping activity. Such activities may include simply carrying field guides or other materials for the ranger or guide, helping with cleanup activities or habitat restoration, or designing and producing a pamphlet or video on a park resource issue.[24]

Other programs encourage the use of vacation time to volunteer in parks. Programs at Cape Cod National Seashore involve both regional and international volunteers who may use vacation time for several days or weeks to assist the park in various resource conservation projects. Participants in such programs have replanted beach grass on sensitive barrier beach areas and constructed wheelchair-accessible boardwalks through fragile wetlands.[25]

Press Releases, Media Packets, and Feature Articles

These can be a powerful and effective means of reaching the public. Press releases can be devised to serve different functions. They can be used to inform the media about important matters deserving their attention or they can serve as "copy" for direct use in media articles or presentations. Press releases should be clear, concise, factual, and easy to comprehend and written at different levels or in different ways to reach specific target audiences.

Feature articles can also be a powerful means of getting important resource messages to various audiences. Articles in publications by the National Geographic Society, Audubon Society, major news magazines, and others can bring broad-scale issues such as air quality and biological diversity concerns to wide audiences. The results of mutual effort in this area can be quite effective. It is advantageous to have a well-informed park staff member on call to be interviewed when opportunities arise.[26]

Web Sites, New Media, and Related Programs

The Greater Yellowstone Science Learning Center Web site is a stellar example of an educational Web site that integrates science information and educational reference materials.[27]

As noted earlier, Views of the National Parks is a web-based educational package on individual parks and related resource subjects and topics. Modules on biological diversity, wilderness, and other subjects offer educators and individuals a means for learning about these subjects in an interactive electronic format.[28]

The NPS Web Ranger Program is also an interactive web-based program that offers park resource–related activates to children. The program is reaching over 50,000 individuals worldwide. Modules on coral reefs, climate change, and a variety of other subjects are offered through this program.[29]

It is important to remember that Internet-based programs sometimes can have limited outreach capabilities (similar to the concern expressed earlier about defaulting to using brochures as the primary means of communication). Internet-based programs require that users select the site or location they wish to view. In some cases, target audiences that need to be reached may not be interested in (or drawn to) a website or related Internet-based product on that topic. Hence, although Internet-based programs and activities are increasingly important and useful, care must be taken to assure that they are indeed reaching the groups and individuals in need of being informed and in the quantity needed to generate appropriate resource protection solutions. Websites, new media, and other related approaches are an important part of the overall mix. Designing these products so that they are attractive, compelling, accurate, motivational, and appropriate can generate positive "viral" re-distribution.[30]

Websites Referenced

1. http://www.nps.gov/history/history/online_books/brochures
2. http://www.nature.nps.gov/climatechange/docs/NPSClimateChangeBrochure.pdf
   http://www.nps.gov/history/history/index.htm
3. http://www.nps.gov/pore/parkmgmt/upload/rps_invasiveplants_and_horsemanure_060718.pdf
4. http://www.nationalparks.org/discover-parks/index.cfm?fa=viewPark&pid=BELA
5. http://www.nps.gov/olym/parknews/olympic-national-park-newsletter.htm
6. http://www.nps.gov/hfc/products/waysides/index.htm
   http://www.nps.gov/hfc/products/waysides/way-samples.htm
7. http://www.ucmp.berkeley.edu/exhibits/biomes/forests.php
   http://www.amnh.org/exhibitions/climatechange/?section=ice
8. http://www.amnh.org/traveling/exhibitions/climate.php?gclid=CPOOssnQgKYCFcfe4AodzEN4og
9. http://www.nps.gov/aboutus/oil-spill-response.htm
10. http://www.nps.gov/grba/naturescience/lightscape.htm
    http://www.nps.gov/nabr/parknews/news040507.htm
    http://www.nps.gov/dewa/forkids/upload/sb6JrSpace.pdf
11. http://www.msnbc.msn.com/id/3032619/vp/28003636#28003636
12. http://www.nps.gov/nr/twhp/descrip.htm
13. http://inside.nps.gov/index.cfm?handler=viewnpsnewsarticle&type=Announcements&id=9585
14. http://www.projectwet.org
15. http://www.nationalparks.org/npf-at-work/mission

16. http://nature.nps.gov/views

17. http://www.nationalparks.org/npf-at-work/our-programs/electronic-field-trip

18. http://www.nps.gov/learn/trt

19. http://www.nature.nps.gov/multimedia/gwseries/georgewright.cfm

20. http://ngm.nationalgeographic.com/2008/11/light-pollution/klinkenborg-text

21. http://www.pbs.org/nationalparks/people
    http://www.cbc.ca/documentarychannel/subscribe.html

22. http://www.nature.nps.gov/multimedia/Ocean1/index.cfm

23. http://www.nps.gov/blca/forteachers/outreachpartners.htm
    http://www.nature.nps.gov/multimedia/gwseries/getinvolved.cfm

24. http://inside.nps.gov/index.cfm?handler=viewnpsnewsarticle&type=Announcements&id=9585

25. http://www.nationalgeographic.com/field/projects/bioblitz.html

26. http://www.msnbc.msn.com/id/3032619/vp/28004734#28004734
    http://channel.nationalgeographic.com/channel/great-migrations
    http://www.nature.nps.gov/multimedia/OilSpillEVER/index.cfm

27. http://www.nps.gov/yell/planyourvisit/resourceandissues.htm
    http://greateryellowstonescience.org

28. http://nature.nps.gov/views

29. http://www.nps.gov/webrangers

30. http://www.nature.nps.gov/biology/migratoryspecies

Conclusion

Resource management and interpretation have been interconnected since their inception. Over time great advancements have been made within each field. Interpreters have broadened the value of parks by reaching out to underserved audiences, embracing civic engagement concepts, and incorporating social science findings into their day-to-day practices. Resource managers have elevated the use of sound science to enable park management to make appropriate decisions related to protecting sensitive resources and to achieve desired future conditions.

As our technological and industrialized world both shrinks and speeds up, noted park historian Bill Brown once remarked, parks and protected areas are increasingly becoming "islands of hope." They save the best of what we as humans have to offer, and they save the best of what nature has to offer. But they are also potentially becoming islands of isolation, at risk of being overwhelmed by external adverse influences. The time has come for resource managers and interpreters to again work in tandem to engage citizens in enjoying, understanding, appreciating, and protecting our society's most treasured protected resources. It may take a village to educate a child, but, likewise, it takes a multitude of partners to save a park.

As our technological and industrialized world both shrinks and speeds up, parks and protected areas are increasingly becoming "islands of hope."

As stated earlier, with this in mind, traditional time-honored interpretive techniques can shine in this regard. For example, interpreters are capable of bringing out the awe and splendor of the night sky, the impressive size and distance of distant stars and galaxies, the magnitude of space, the miracle of a "living" planet Earth when seen from space. They can also remind us of Earth's visible systems and patterns. Similarly, reconnecting visitors with the awesomeness of natural soundscapes can bring comprehension, as well as a call to action. The spine-chilling howls of a wolf that break the deep quiet of a starry night, the muffled but permeating hoot-hoot-hoot of an owl, the hushed voices and the crackling of a cheerful campfire, and a volley of rifle fire at a Civil War site are elemental and memorable moments that last a lifetime.

As it was in the beginning of the national park experiment, combining sound science with resonating interpretation is needed more than ever for safeguarding and perpetuating our most treasured natural and cultural resources. If and when we are intertwined and united on this front, we can accomplish this. History and precedent have proven so, and both are on our side.

Applying Communications Solutions to Current Resource Issues and Situations

Now is your opportunity to practice how you would develop customized communications assistance for the following ongoing resource protection issues. In each case, fill in the matrix with your carefully crafted determinations of the essential ingredients necessary to affect successful resource issue communications. (Visit http://www.nature.nps.gov/educationoutreach/interpretivesolutions.)

Potential Case Studies

Night Sky

- http://www.darksky.org/mc/page.do;jsessionid=4FBEE0D9F5C14D72C7370E1F2BC72CA6.mc1?sitePageId=55060
- http://ngm.nationalgeographic.com/2008/11/light-pollution/klinkenborg-text

Natural Sound

- http://www.nature.nps.gov/naturalsounds/
- http://www.nature.nps.gov/parkscience/index.cfm?IssueID=21

Ocean stewardship

- http://communities.earthportal.org/ncseoceans2011/

Biodiversity

- http://www.dlia.org
- http://www.nature.nps.gov/biology
- http://www.npca.org/wildlife_protection/biodiversity/report

Native plants (and difficulties caused by invasives)

- http://www.nature.nps.gov/biology/invasivespecies
- http://www.invasivespeciesinfo.gov/

Endangered species (including recovery successes and ongoing efforts)

http://www.nature.nps.gov/biology/endangeredspecies

http://www.everglades.national-park.com/info.htm

http://www.shenandoah.national-park.com/nat.htm

California Condor restoration

http://www.nps.gov/pinn/naturescience/condors.htm

http://www.SFGate.com

Resource Issue Interpretive Matrix

Essential Steps for Facilitating the Resource Issue Interpretive Component Development Process

<table>
<tr><th colspan="2">Step One: Identify the Issue and Relevant Human Dimension Factors</th></tr>
<tr><td>Critical Resource Issue</td><td>Clearly articulate the issue (preferably in 100 words or fewer).
The interpretive effort should address a specific critical resource issue, its root cause, and potential solutions.</td></tr>
<tr><td>Human Dimension Component</td><td>Identify the role humans play in the resource issue (both in creating the problem and/or resolving the issue).
Is the human dimension factor high, medium, or low? If the human dimension factor is low, then possibly only limited interpretive involvement may be needed. If it is high, the interpretive effort may need to be extensive.</td></tr>
<tr><th colspan="2">Step Two: Identify the Target Audience(s)</th></tr>
<tr><td>Target Audience</td><td>Identify the target audience and why they are important to reach.
What role do they play in stabilizing, improving, or resolving the issue?

Programs that address critical resources should target specific, appropriate audiences including, but not limited to:
• Internal Park Staff
• Park Partners
• Traditional Visitors
• Concessionaires
• Park Neighbors
• Schools
• Local Businesses
• Other Agencies
• Ranchers
• Tribal Members
• Hunters or Anglers</td></tr>
<tr><th colspan="2">Step Three: Determine the Message</th></tr>
<tr><td>Message/Theme</td><td>Clearly articulate the specific message you want to get across (in 50 words or fewer if possible).</td></tr>
<tr><td>Interpretive Intent</td><td>Determine the purpose of your message.
Is it to gain support? To change behavior? To simply inform? To instill appreciation? To resolve a human impact?</td></tr>
</table>

continued on next page

Step Four: Select the Appropriate Interpretive Approaches or Techniques	
Media/Methods Description and Summary	Select the media/method used to deliver the message(s) to each target audience. Recognize that specific audiences may receive information in different ways. A variety of techniques should be considered, including, but not limited to: • Brochures • Maps • Signs • Videos • Live Presentations • Displays • Public Meetings • Guidebooks • Broadcast Media • Electronic Resources • Posters • Personnel at School Programs • Commercial and Agency Radio Spots • TV or Other Periodicals • Movies or Short Film
Other Essential Ingredients	
Budget	Estimate cost of materials, development and shipping, graphic design/artwork, installation/set-up or distribution, personal services, and staff time commitment.
Collaborative Partners	Identify interpretive specialist(s) from the park, regional office, national office, and/or partner organizations who are able to collaborate on the Interpretive Component.
Evaluation	Determine strategies to evaluate the success of the interpretive product. What is the desired future/outcome? Use established interpretive evaluation processes, as well as resource condition assessment indicators.

Additional Acknowledgements

Appreciation is extended to the many additional individuals who provided editing and content review. Included within this group are NPS Natural Resource Office of Education and Outreach employees Virginia Reams, Jeff Selleck, Sara Melena, Lynne Murdock, and student assistant Erin Drake, whose input, editorial assistance, and advice were invaluable. Charles Beall, chief of interpretation at North Coast Cascades National Park, and Christopher Stein, former chief of interpretation at Yosemite National Park, also offered input and reviews. Additional appreciation goes to Dayton Duncan, who co-produced the "National Parks: America's Best Idea" series, and long-time affiliates Tim Merriman and George Price, who engaged in many spirited park preservation and interpretation discussions over the years. Also to be thanked are the many individuals who provided thoughts, ideas and concepts that contributed to this publication. Included with these ranks are Jeri Hall, who pioneered the Resource Protection Interdisciplinary Team project; Dr. Tim Carruthers, with the University of Maryland Integration and Application Network program; Dr. Dan Decker, director of the Cornell University Human Dimensions Research Unit; Interpretive Specialist John Morris; Paul Olig John Day Fossil Beds Chief of Interpretation; Dr. Peter Dratch, natural resources colleague and former journalist; Jana Friesen McCabe, writer editor Yosemite National Park; Elizabeth Munding, writer editor, Yosemite National Park; Dr. Gary Davis, retired NPS marine ecologist; Dr. Mietek Kolipinski, NPS Pacific West Region; Tom Richter, Midwest Region Chief of Interpretation; Bill Brown, retired NPS historian; Mike DeBacker, Heartland I&M Network coordinator; Greg Kudray, Pacific Islands I&M coordinator; Jim Gale, Hawaii Volcanoes Chief of Interpretation; Glen Kaye, retired Intermountain Region Chief of Interpretation; Sallie Beavers, Kaloko Honokohau National Historical Park; Sherry Middlemis-Brown Herbert Hoover National Historic Site; and Joanne Blacoe who assisted with editing related interpretive policy materials. Likewise, it is important to acknowledge the parks themselves, particularly Sequoia Kings Canyon National Park, and its inspirational majestic giant Sequoias (where the author served as a horseback ranger in his early days with the National Park

Service); Cape Cod National Seashore, with its amazing interplay of cultural and natural features (where the author served as South District interpreter and park historian); Morristown National Historical Park, with its moving human and natural survival story (where the author served as chief of interpretation during the Bicentennial); and Yosemite National Park, with its beautiful sunsets (where the author learned from his mom at an early age how to appreciate the out-of-doors and national parks in particular).

References

Aronchick, D. 1991. A Research Project to Aid in the Development of Targeted Environmental Messages for the Canadian Parks Service. Business Generation Group, Ottawa, Ontario.

Brochu, L., and T. Merriman. 2002. Personal Interpretation: Connecting Your Audience to Heritage Resources. National Association of Interpretation, Fort Collins, Colorado.

Brockman, C. F. 1978. Park Naturalists and the Evolution of NPS Interpretation. Journal of Forest History. Forest History Society, Santa Cruz, California.

Brown, B. F. 1979. Interpretation: A Brain-Compatible Way to Learn. The Interpretation Research Institute, Ann Arbor, Michigan.

Brown, B. F. 1979. Interpretation: A Brain-Compatible Way to Learn. The Interpretation Research Institute, Ann Arbor, Michigan.

Brown, W.E. 1971. Islands of Hope. National Park and Recreation Association, Washington, DC.

Bruce, H. 1992. Will Ecotourism Save Atlantic Canada? Commercial News, Halifax, Nova Scotia.

Bryant, H. C., and W. W. Atwood, Jr. 1932. Research and Education in the National Parks. U.S. National Park Service, Washington, D.C.

Buggey, S. 1991. Managing Landscapes in the Canadian Parks Service. Cultural Resource Management Bulletin 14(6). U.S. National Park Service, Washington, D.C.

Cahn, R. 1985. Horace Albright Remembers. National Parks Conservation Association 59(9–10):27.

Canada, Department of Environment. 1990. Canada's Green Plan. Environment Canada, Ottawa, Ontario.

Canada, Department of the Environment. 1990. State of the Parks Profiles. Environment Canada, Ottawa, Ontario.

Canada, Department of the Environment. 1990. State of the Parks Report. Environment Canada, Ottawa, Ontario.

Chase, A. 1987. How to Save Our National Parks. The Atlantic Monthly 260(1):35.

Corbett, J. 2006. Communicating Nature: How We Create and Understand Environmental Messages. Island Press. Washington, D.C.

Corbett, J.B. & Durfee, J.L. 2004. Testing public (un)certainty of science: Media representations of global warming. Science Communication, 26(2), 129-151.

Cox, R. 2006. Environmental Communication and the Public Sphere. Sage Publications Inc. Thousand Oaks, California.

Cunningham, R. L. 1984. Interpretation of Natural Resource Management in the NPS. U.S. National Park Service. Western Region, San Francisco.

Davis, S. 1992. What Canada is Doing. Courier 37(1). U.S. National Park Service, Washington, D.C.

Doucette, J. E., and D. N. Cole. 1993. Wilderness Visitor Education: Information About Alternative Techniques. U.S. Forest Service, Ogden, Utah.

Durfee, J.L. 2006. "Social change" and "status quo" framing effects on risk perception: An exploratory experiment. Science Communication, 27(4), 459-495.

Durfee, J. L. & Corbett, J.B. 2005. Context and controversy: Global warming coverage. Nieman Reports, 59(4), 88-89.

Fazio, J. R. 1975. Liberty Hyde Bailey and Enos A. Mills. Nature Study, University of Idaho.

Field, D. R.., and J. A. Wagar. 1973. Visitor Groups and Interpretation in Parks and Other Outdoor Settings. Journal of Environmental Education 5(1):41.

Follows, D. 1988. Resource Interpretation. Heritage Communicator 2(3):14. Calgary, Alberta.

Gensler, G. 1977. The Role of Interpretation in Park Management. College of Forest Resources, University of Washington.

Goethe, C. M. 1960. Nature Study in National Parks Movement. Yosemite Nature Notes 39(7):9. Yosemite National Park, California.

Gregg, W. P., Jr. Summer 1985. Biosphere Reserves. Orion 4(3). Myrin Institute, Fort Lee, New Jersey.

Ham, S. H., B. Weiler, M. Hughes, T. J. Brown, J. Curtis, and M. Poll. 2008. Asking visitors to help: Research to guide strategic communication for protected area management. Gold Coast, Australia: Sustain Tourism Cooperative Research Centre.

Hanna, J. W. 1975. Interpretive Skills for Environmental Communicators. Department of Recreation and Parks, Texas A and M University, College Station, Texas.

Harris, B. 1992. National Parks of Canada. Smith Books, Toronto.

Hester, F. E. 1991. Nature's Laboratories. National Parks Conservation Association 65(1–2):18.

Hummel, M. 1989. Endangered Spaces: The Future For Canada's Wilderness. Key Porter Books Ltd., Ontario.

Jacobson, S. K. 2009. Communication Skills for Conservation Professionals, 2nd Edition. Island Press. Washington, D.C.

Jacobson, S. K., M. D. McDuff, and M. C. Monroe. 2006. Conservation Education and Outreach Techniques. Oxford University Press. Oxford, England.

Johnson, D. 1986. The Role and Responsibility of Interpretation. University of Washington.

Larsen, D. L. 2003. Meaningful Interpretation: How to Connect Hearts and Minds to Places, Objects and other Resources. Eastern National Park and Monument Association, Philadelphia, Pennsylvania.

Lewis, W. J. 1981. Interpreting for Park Visitors. Eastern National Park and Monument Association, Philadelphia, Pennsylvania.

Machlis, G. E., editor. 1986. Interpretive Views. National Park and Conservation Association, Washington, D.C.

Mackintosh, B. 1986. Interpretation in the National Park Service. National Park Service, Washington, D.C.

Mackintosh, B. 1992. Interpretation: A Tool for N.P.S. Expansion. Interpretation Winter:10. U.S. National Park Service, Washington, D.C..

McCarthy, J. 1989. Nature Conservation in the U.S. and Canada. Legacy 13(3):1. National Association of Interpretation, Fort Collins, Colorado.

McKendry, J. 1988. Interpretation: Key to the Park Experience. National Parks and Conservation Association, Washington, D.C.

McMillan, S.L., and F.J. Eagles. 1991. An Evaluation of Formal Evening Programs in the Ontario Provincial Parks. Department of Recreation and Leisure Studies, University of Waterloo, Ontario.

Merriman, T., and L. Brochu. 2005. Management of Interpretive Sites: Developing Sustainable Operations Through Effective Leadership. National Association of Interpretation, Fort Collins, Colorado.

Meyer, K., and S. Thomas. 1991. Designing Your Wilderness Education Action Plan. U.S. Department of Agriculture, Washington, D.C.

Miller, L. H. 1960. The Nature Guide Movement in National Parks. Yosemite Nature Notes 39(7):12. Yosemite National Park, California.

Mills, E. 1990 (revised). Adventures of a Nature Guide. New Past Press, Friendship, Wisconsin.

Mullins, G. W., and M. Watson. 1992. Interpreting Critical Resource Issues in National Parks: An Assessment. School of Natural Resources, Ohio State University, Columbus, Ohio.

Mullins, G. W., J. Peine, W. Gregg, S. Canter, and K. Tassier. 1987. Interpreting Man and the Biosphere Concepts in U.S. National Parks. U.S. National Park Service, Washington, D.C.

Nabhan, G.P. 1989. Enduring Seeds. North Point Press, Berkeley, California.

National Association for Interpretation. 1993. M. Whatley and Oxman. Pages 347–350 in Proceedings of Successfully Interpreting Critical Resource Issues in U.S. and Canadian National Parks. Madison, Wisconsin.

O'Riordan, T., and C. Wood. 1992. Landscapes for Tomorrow. Yorkshire Dales National Park Commission, Yorkshire Dales, U.K.

Oxman, H. and D. Clarke. 1993 Environmental Citizenship: Inside Out. Environment Canada, Ottawa.

Peine, J. 1987. Smokies Study Visitor Communications. Park Science 8(2):6. U.S. National Park Service, Seattle, Washington.

Peine, J. D., C. A. Walker, and P. H. Motts. 1984. Evaluating Communications with Visitors to Great Smoky Mountains National Park. U.S. National Park Service Southeast Region, Great Smoky Mountains National Park, Gatlinburg, Tennessee.

Ralston, C. August 1981. Interpreters: 65th Anniversary. U.S. National Park Service, Washington, D.C.

Ricou, T. J. 1993. The Nature of Canada: A Primer on Spaces and Species. Environment Canada, Ottawa, Ontario.

Roggenbuck, J. W. 1992. Use of Persuasion to Reduce Resource Impacts and Visitor Conflicts. Sagamore Publishing, Champaign, Illinois.

Russell, C. 1960. Yosemite: A 40th Anniversary. Yosemite Nature Notes 39(7). Yosemite National Park, California.

Sax, J. L. 1976. America's National Parks. Natural History 85(8).

Smith, G. A., and D. R. Williams, editors. 1999. Ecological Education in Action. State University of New York. Albany, New York.

Standish, R. I. 1985. Information Folders for National Parks. National Recreation and Park Association, Washington, D.C. p. 18.

Sudia, T. W. 1985. National Parks and Domestic. Washington, D.C.

Thompson, J.L. 2008. Interdisciplinary research team dynamics: A systems approach to understanding communication and collaboration in complex teams. Saarbruecken, Germany: VDM Verlag Publishing.

Thompson, J.L., Forster, C.B., Werner, C., & Peterson, T.R. 2010. Mediated Modeling: Using Collaborative Processes to Integrate Scientist and Stakeholder Knowledge about Greenhouse Gas Emissions in an Urban Ecosystem. Society & Natural Resources, 23(8).

Thompson, J.L. 2009. Building collective communication competence in interdisciplinary research teams. Journal of Applied Communication Research, 37(3), 278-297.

Tilden, F. 1957. Interpreting Our Heritage. University of North Carolina Press, Chapel Hill, North Carolina.

U.S. National Park Service. 1994. Interpreting Global Change: A National Park Service Communicator's Handbook. Washington, D.C.

U.S. National Park Service. 1994. Report on Natural Resource Issues Interpretation in the National Park Service. Washington, D.C.

U.S. National Park Service. 1964. Service History. Horace M. Albright Training Center, Grand Canyon, Arizona.

Whatley, M. E. 1995. Interpreting Critical Natural Resource in Canadian and United States National Park Service Areas. Natural Resources Report NPS/NRCACO/NRR-95/17. U.S. National Park Service, Denver, CO.

Whatley, M. E., and W. Springer. 1989. Critical Resource Issues: Training. Legacy 13(2). National Association of Interpretation, Fort Collins, Colorado.

Whatley, M. E., and W. Springer. 1988. Interpreting Critical Resource Issues: Training. Interpretation. U.S. National Park Service, Washington, D.C.

Winter, L. 1993. Bridging the Communications Gap: Linking Interpreters, Resource Managers, and Researchers. Park Science 13(3):9–10. U.S. National Park Service, Seattle, Washington.

About the Author

Michael (Mike) Whatley began his career in interpretation and resource stewardship over 40 years ago. Family trips to Yosemite motivated him to obtain a bachelor of science in environmental resources from Sacramento State University. While enrolled there, he became an intern with the East Bay Regional Park District, attended the University of Uppsala Sweden during his junior year, and obtained student-career status with the National Park Service. He obtained a masters in wildland resource sciences at the University of California, Berkeley.

Mike's early NPS career took him to Lake Mead National Recreation Area as a law enforcement ranger; Sequoia-Kings Canyon National Park as a patrol ranger, horseback ranger, and naturalist; Albright Training Center in Grand Canyon National Park as a liaison; and the NPS Southern Arizona Group Office, where he undertook short assignments at Canyon de Chelly, Fort Bowie, Tumacaccori, and Saguaro. Mike served as the park's chief of interpretation, historian, and public information officer at Morristown National Historical Park, and after that spent more than 20 years at Cape Cod National Seashore. While at Cape Cod, he became a lead instructor for the North Atlantic Region interpretive skills team, authored a series of publications, supervised an extensive interpretation and environmental education operation, and received the regional Freeman Tilden Award for excellence in interpretation. Currently Mike serves as the chief of the Office of Education and Outreach within the NPS Natural Resource Stewardship and Science Directorate. Over the duration of his career Mike has participated in a number of international assignments, including travels to Jordan, Israel, China, and Canada and has taught at the college level including at University of Northern Colorado and Colorado State University. Mike is a Life Member of the National Association for Interpretation and the George Melendez Wright Society.

Mike is married to his wonderfully supportive wife Kareen, has an inspirational daughter Jennifer, and grandchildren, all of whom enjoy and appreciate parks and open places and love connecting with their recently rekindled Hawaiian heritage (thanks to Kareen's genealogical skills).